450

Basketball's

Explosive Inside Power Game

DEDICATION

As is so often stated, behind every man stands a great woman; I have been especially fortunate in this department. The marvelous woman in my life is my wife, Polly Ann, who has shared my life, the long hours, the hard work, the peaks and the valleys with equanimity, plus having three children—Russ, Dale, and Debbie. Last but not by any means least is my mother, Hilda McCready, a better mom a son never had.

ACKNOWLEDGEMENTS

Dr. P. J. Emma, principal Montgomery Blair High School, for his sincere encouragement and continuous support.

Mr. Bill Kyle, Director of Athletics for the Montgomery County school system, who has contributed so much to my career; Jim Kehoe, former teacher, coach, and Athletic Director of the University of Maryland, for teaching me dedication through hard work; H. A. "Bud" Millikan, former coach University of Maryland, for teaching me the importance of fundamentals; "Lefty" Driesell, coach University of Maryland, who has given me his advice and help when needed; Bill Foster, Duke University, for his thoughts on and insights into basketball; Dave Smalley, United States Naval Academy coach—women, for all of his sincere help over the years through thick and thin; Herman Rubenstein, owner Buffalo Gap Basketball Camp, for getting me started and steering me straight; Warren Crutchfield and Hank Mallory, my assistant coaches, for adding immeasurably to the success of my teams; to my twin brother, Jack, who consistently pushed me to a greater effort and has always been there when needed; and to Eddie Crane, reporter for the Washington Star, for his constant help to so many high school athletic programs. Special thanks to Lyn Pusey, Sports Editor of the *Montgomery Journal*, who has been so enthusiastic and supportive to me.

My most grateful appreciation goes to all those wonderful young men who played for me during the past 18 years. It is their tremendous effort, loyalty, and hard work that has given me something to write about.

Basketball's

Explosive Inside Power Game

Gene Doane

Parker Publishing Company • West Nyack, New York

Library of Congress Cataloging in Publication Data

Doane, Gene
    Basketball's explosive inside power game.

    1. Basketball--Offense. I. Title.
GV889.D6   796.32'32   78-13035
ISBN 0-13-072181-6

Printed in the United States of America

Multiple Advantages

of This Offense

For years I have strived, as have other coaches, to implement a simplified offense, one capable of measuring up to any defensive change of concept. The foundation for the Explosive Inside Power Offense is the movement of all players to different floor positions in simple moves. While there are set options or patterns, concepts are taught to enable the players to take advantage of opportunities presented by the defense. The Explosive Inside Power Offense is based on recognition of what the defense is trying to do and where its men are positioned—an important difference from a set pattern, which has to be run regardless of what the defense is doing.

Nothing causes the defense more problems than inside movement and movement with screening. By constantly applying pressure at the point of attack, you are not allowing the defense to reorganize itself, but rather, you are taking away the defensive man's ability to anticipate his man's move.

You may incorporate any offensive pattern in this offense. The important thing is that your players will not predetermine their moves, while at the same time they will still be functioning in a structured atmosphere.

The Explosive Inside Power Offense can be adapted to all tempos of play because it allows adjustments to be made each year as your personnel changes without changing the basic concept of your offense.

This book demonstrates the Explosive Inside Power style of play. The material is presented in a form that is easy to follow. The how's, why's, and what's are not left out but organized in a step-by-step explanation. Coaches at any level will find the material helpful and adaptable to their situations.

Regardless of the style of basketball you are currently using, this book will supply new and exciting options to improve your team's offensive scoring punch. The basic concept of this book is that of having a play option designed to fit the abilities of each individual player.

In Chapter 1 the Inside Power Game is developed. The criteria for utilizing this offense are explained simply in step-by-step fashion.

Chapter 2 shows how to utilize a good point guard. The point guard series takes advantage of your guard's passing and penetrating abilities. Should you be blessed with a tall point guard, there are options for his size advantage.

Chapters 5 and 6 will be of great interest to the coach who has one or two big men on his squad. Our 2 and 5 plays were developed for these players. The power roll series, the low double screen series, and the open side drive series may be used as an integral part of your present system.

Chapter 1 is for the shooter. The 3 play series, or the 34 play as we call it, when run to the opposite side of the floor, affords tremendous opportunities for your outside shooters. In Chapter 4 our 4 play series, or 43 to the opposite side of floor, is designed for the qualities of your small forward or additional shooter.

The inside rotation series against zone defenses in Chapters 7 and 8 is another dynamic feature of the book. This quick hitting zone attack will drive opponents out of their zone defenses. Offensive basketball from endline to endline is stressed in Chapter 9.

Each chapter concludes with important drills to facilitate the teaching of the various offensive series described in the chapter. By giving you the specifics, I have attempted to detail the Explosive Inside Power Game as it developed and is utilized today. My purpose in these pages is to provoke thought and to present my concepts of aggressive winning basketball.

Gene Doane

Table of Contents

1

Requirements for the Explosive Inside Power Game

Winning has been described as scoring more points than your opponents. The best way to accomplish this is through a system of organized team play. An offensive system that divides the scoring potential equally is much better than one attuned to one or two players.

The ability to score varies with each player and, in turn, with every team. I believe this is more true in junior and senior high school, where you must develop the talents of each player coming to your school. Some players are better outside shooters, others are better at the short shot, and still others are better at the penetration drive. But there is one area they all can excel in—the close-in shot. You must try to equalize the abilities of your players, and close-in shots build the confidence of even the poorer shooters.

With this in mind, we developed the Inside Power Game. We wanted scoring opportunities to develop close to the basket. We wanted to bring the maximum scoring opportunity to all five players within the foul line—15 feet from the basket. This restricted area must be penetrated with ball and player movement. At the same time, we wanted to have as much down screening in our offense as possible. Diagram 1-1 illustrates what is meant by the term down screen. The defensive man must closely guard your offensive player in this position, so he is easy to screen. Since we feel the down screen is very difficult to play defense against, we want to incorporate it into the offensive flow.

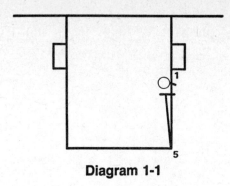

Diagram 1-1

Use of this approach led us to further specialization within our offensive game. When working to enhance the strengths of your players and hide their shortcomings, you should not overlook the area of substitutions. How are you utilizing your bench strength? We feel a player coming off the bench should be a specialist. He will generally have a specific job to do and must be a specialist in that job.

THE BASIC CRITERION
FOR A SOUND OFFENSE—SIMPLICITY

Our thinking has always been directed toward keeping things simple. Too many inexperienced coaches waste too much time doodling up fancy offenses and defenses when they should be concentrating on the simple elements that lead to success. If you can accomplish ball and man movement with one pass, so much the better. An example of a successful but simple play is our 4 play, described in detail in Chapter 4. The 4 play was designed to put tremendous pressure on the defense close to the basket in the simplest way possible, by having two players there. Then we just play fundamental basketball. It is much simpler to drill into your players a few simple rules that they can respond to instinctively. Throughout our system of play we want each player to be able to respond to the basic moves of our opponents. It is best to keep things clearly defined and free of extras.

RELATIONSHIP OF OFFENSE TO DEFENSE

Offensive theory must blend with defensive theory. Since we play a physical man-to-man offense, our defense is of the same nature. This no-frills approach is incorporated into our entire system. One phase should complement the other in any system used.

Floor balance is of critical importance to your defensive posture. This is a vital area in which we are all too often remiss. Our philosophy is going to dictate to us how many offensive men we are willing to send to the boards. Since our philosophy in defense is summed up best by three words—get the ball—on offense this same line of thinking should follow. We send four men to the offensive boards and only one man back for defensive purposes. Our purpose is to *get the ball*! We have found it to be to our advantage to crash the offensive boards aggressively. We believe it helps our defense by minimizing our opponent's fastbreak. When you obtain extra shots, you are helping control the tempo of the game.

The Inside Power Game allows you to control game tempo by getting the high percentage shot. When you attain the good shot and rebound aggressively, the pressure on your opponent's defense is immense. This, in turn, allows your team to play defense with greater intensity. The tempo can be fast, slow, or somewhere in between, but it will be what you desire, not what your opponent desires. Every move from then on is fundamental basketball, and fundamental basketball is like a chess game, except a bit quicker. Each side knows what the other's moves are, but the team that is the quickest to react will counter the other's moves. I repeat—keep it simple.

PRACTICE TO BE PERFECT

Practice should be limited to the fundamentals but performed with great intensity. In other words, it should be a reflection of your philosophy. Winning teams practice harder than losing teams. Every practice session must be highly organized, and every drill must have a definite purpose directly related to your offense. Each session should be timed and no longer than ten minutes. The concentration time span on any particular drill practiced with intensity is not much over ten minutes. If you must practice longer, come back later in your practice schedule for ten more minutes.

ADVANTAGES OF THE POINT OR ONE GUARD FRONT

We use the one guard offense for several reasons. It is difficult to double team due to the distance between wing and point positions.

With most high school teams, it is easier to find and develop one superior ball-handling guard than two. The added area your point guard has to operate in, plus the advantage of four entry points, allows for greater flexibility. This is another advantage of the one guard front.

To me, the point guard is the most important position on the team. The point guard is an extension of the coach. He is the one who puts into action the coach's teachings. The successful teams all have a good playmaker; without one, few are successful.

FLEXIBILITY OF PERSONNEL

Flexibility of personnel is one of the most important things you can have. At the junior and senior high school levels, where you adapt to what you have, flexibility is critical. Players, however, tend to fall into several categories, at least this has been my observation over my coaching career.

Players generally fall into three types. The first type is the 5'6" to 6' player. He can be either quick or slow but is generally your best shooter and ball handler. The second type is the 6'1" to 6'3" player, who again is either quick or of average speed. He will generally be a fine shooter or an aggressive rebounder and defensive player. The third type is the 6'4" to 6'7" player, who you are forced to play in the post position. If you have more than two, you have a natural big forward. Personally, I have never been afforded that luxury.

The Inside Power Game affords you the ability to mix these combinations to their best advantages. You are then able to play to their strengths.

INCREASING THE REBOUNDING EDGE

Teaching your players their offensive rebounding assignments is very simple from the 1-3-1 set. As noted earlier in this chapter, we send four players to the offensive boards at all times. We feel this is statistically sound since most high school teams will miss 55 to 60 percent of the time. All of these misses will be up for grabs, and we intend to grab them.

Since the players will have no way of knowing which shots will be missed, they must *assume that every shot will be missed*. Statistically, more fouls occur on the second and third shots, so the opportunity for a three-point play is increased with every offensive rebound.

Most important to our way of thinking is the ability of each player to recognize when his teammate is about to shoot. The key word here is "about." A successful offensive rebounder must be going aggressively to the boards a split second before the shot is taken. In the Inside Power Game each player knows exactly when his teammate will be shooting and from where. With intelligent anticipation, the offensive player can get the jump on the defense.

INITIATING THE OFFENSE WITH MOVEMENT KEYS

Our offensive thinking is to initiate the offense as simply and quickly as possible, while eliminating any misunderstandings as to the option being run. This is accomplished by the point guard's movement in the following manner:

1. Pass and cut in the direction of the pass down the lane (vertical cut) and then
   a. Opposite ball
   b. Ball-side
   (See Diagram 1-2.)
2. Pass and come to the ball. (See Diagram 1-3.)
3. Dribble to wing position of the 3 or 4 man. (See Diagram 1-4.)

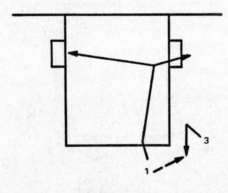

Diagram 1-2

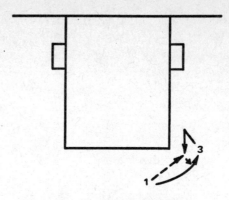

Diagram 1-3

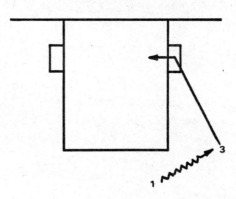

Diagram 1-4

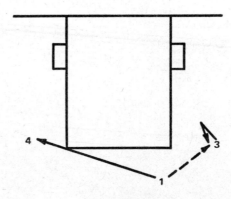

Diagram 1-5

4. Pass and cut away (angle cut to wing position opposite pass). (See Diagram 1-5.)

5. Vocal communication with movement key. This last item can be helpful to the coach who has a very young, inexperienced team. We use vocal communication whenever possible to help eliminate mistakes.

PERSONNEL REQUIREMENTS BY POSITION

The Point Guard—1 Man

The point guard or 1 man is the offensive quarterback for us. Our success is highly dependent upon his success. Since he is an extension of the coach on the floor, he should be a leader.

Size, while desired, is not the primary prerequisite. We have had point guards vary in size from 5'6" to 6'3". Our main concern is that he be highly respected by the other players, be a leader, and be able to control the tempo of the game.

The point guard has to be a good ball-handler. It is here you benefit by needing to develop only one playmaker. The point guard's ability to read the opponent's defensive coverages directly affects your team's success against various defenses. In later chapters you will see how this system is developed. Since the point guard has the responsibility of getting the ball to each player in his best shooting area, it is important that he be taught in drills conducted under constant pressure.

Whenever possible, we like to have three point guards, preferably one senior, one junior, and one sophomore. In so doing, we have protection at this critical position. We feel it takes two years to develop a point guard, so we use this approach.

The Wing Positions—3 and 4 Men

In this position we want the player with the best perimeter shooting percentage. This player, if we have only one, is designated the 3 man. If you have two exceptional shooters, you can play the strongest rebounder of the two at the 4 position.

Naturally, as coach you want your quickest people playing. We look for speed particularly at the 4 position. It is not essential, though, to have great speed at this position.

Our 4 position (small forward) has been filled by players who ranged from 5'10" to 6'6" in size. The 3 position (shooting guard) has been filled by players varying from 5'9" to 6'5". The important thing here is to be able to fit the personnel into almost any combination the situation demands.

The High Post—5 Man

In the high post position our main concern is the player's ability as a passer, screener, and rebounder. The 5 man is an added source of fire power when he can hit that open 15-footer from the free throw area. Through repeated drills, your 5 man must be taught the drop step and how to take it to the basket, because this is often open for him to drive.

Of your two post men your best passer of the two should play this position. It doesn't matter whether he is the bigger of the two. We generally have someone in the 6'4" to 6'6" range in this position, but there have been years where we have used a 6'1" to 6'3" player. Size helps in this position, but there are other considerations that are more important.

Both post men are taught the basic moves necessary for an effective inside player. They must learn the power moves, turn shot, hook shot, and baby jumper. The 5 man should be your strongest rebounder. He must be taught to be aggressive and to utilize our offensive concept to be an outstanding offensive rebounder.

The 5 man must also be developed into an effective screener since he does so much screening. The Inside Power Offense offers many uses for the talents of an aggressive, tenacious post man. High percentage shooting requires outstanding offensive rebounders.

The Low Post—2 Man

The low post player, by the nature of his location on the court, has to be a strong rebounder. We have used players ranging from 6' to 6'5" here. Our present team uses a 6', 195-pounder here. He was our leading rebounder and second leading scorer, making first team all league. As you can see, we have used average or below-average size players in our post positions.

We teach our 2 man to be an effectual short range (four to eight feet) jump shooter. He must master the inside power moves, drop step, slide bounce step, turn shot, and hook shots. These moves, with the

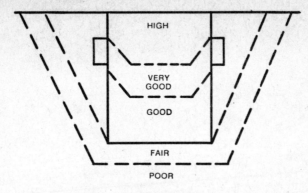

Diagram 1-6

exception of the slide step, are to be mastered without the use of the dribble.

As a rebounder, the 2 man should be drilled in anticipation of his teammate's shot and getting to the proper rebound position, either ball-side or help-side. As a screener, the 2 man must be conscious of the three-second lane and how to properly set various types of screens.

These skills are what we look for in selecting our personnel in tryouts. Our Inside Power Offense was designed with the high percentage shooting areas in mind. Our defense is aimed at keeping our opponents out of these high percentage areas.

As shown in Diagram 1-6, the high percentage area for shooting is the power layup area. What we consider the very good percentage area is the 4- to 8-foot area. Shots taken in this area are the short jumper, hook, and turn shots. The good percentage area is the 10- to 15-foot area, and the fair is the 16- to 21-foot area. To shoot consistently in the area beyond 21 feet is to court disaster. You won't win very often if you shoot from this range.

PLAYER ALIGNMENT AND POSITION IN THE 1-3-1 SET

An essential part of developing a successful team offense is the coach's ability to understand his players' individual abilities and utilize them to their best advantage. A coach should strive for the compatibility of the strengths of his offense with the strengths and weaknesses of his personnel.

Teach the fundamentals, and then you can fit the offense to your

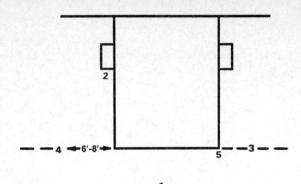

Diagram 1-7

players' abilities. By positioning each player in specific areas, you are creating a better passing angle for your point guard. By numbering each position, you are making it easier to learn. The basic alignment and numbering system is shown in Diagram 1-7.

The 1 man initiates the offense from the top of the circle. At this position he has achieved the proper passing angle to each wing position or post man. The 3 and 4 players should set up 6 to 8 feet from the lane on a line extended through the free throw line. If they receive a pass in this area, they are within 15 to 18 feet from the basket. This is the area from which we want to initiate our perimeter offense. The highest percentage shooting from the perimeter is obtained in this area, and the best passing angles inside occur from this area. We want our 5 man (high post) off-set to the offensive right side, with his foot nearest the 3 man just inside the circle line. He has the option to set to the left side or not, depending on what the defense is showing us that particular night. By positioning him in this off-set position, we feel we have obtained the following advantages:

1. A better angle to screen for the 1 man
2. More open space for penetration by the 1 man to the open side
3. A better down screen angle of the 1 man for the 2, 3, and 4 men
4. Different posture on defense than traditional center alignment
5. 5 man at a better angle to receive passes
6. 5 man given more driving area to the open side he sets up from

The 2 man sets up on the block on a diagonal opposite the 5 man's alignment. This affords an excellent backside rebounding position. We have placed 2 in a position for the close inside high percentage shot. We have placed in this position the strong rebounder who might be a big (6'4" to 6'7"), uncoordinated player. When you have a young player like this who you must use, place him in this area. This is the one area of the floor the defense *must* guard. So if you have a big, awkward kid, here is where you place him, not at the high post.

Since our players play skill positions, they are drilled in the specifics of each position. Shooting drills are designed for the shots they will take in each game. Movement without the ball is an important aspect and is drilled repeatedly. To be an effective teacher you must constantly drill each fundamental.

We want 3 and 4 to receive the ball no higher than the free throw line extended, six to eight feet. By achieving this entry pass, we are in the higher percentage area for shooting, passing, and driving. This gives us the good 45° angle pass to our inside people. Our 3 and 4 players must shape up and face the basket immediately upon catching the ball.

The 3 man is basically our second guard in the sense that he must be able to help bring the ball up the floor against pressure defenses. If you use a third guard in the 4 position, your concern about the ball-handling ability of the 3 man diminishes. The combinations you choose to use at the 3 and 4 positions can change your offensive picture considerably.

THE CONTINUITY OF THE OFFENSE, 1 THROUGH 5 PLAYS

To be successful, any offense must make each play a part of a general flowing pattern made up of several plays, each of which evolves from any other. You will see the evolvement of this concept in the development of each series of plays.

You must always keep in mind the importance of the little things. The details within the offense make the offense go, not the offense itself. These details, repeated over and over again, make for a successful system. In the following chapters each offensive series will be explained in minute detail, followed by the breakdown drills to be utilized in repetitive teaching. The part-whole-part method of teaching is how we tune this fine machine and keep it running smoothly.

2

Developing the Inside Game

3 Play Action Series

BASIC OPTIONS OF THE 3 MAN

This option series developed around the abilities of a good shooting guard. We have had all sizes, from 5'8" to 6'5", play this position. As a group our guards have averaged 54 percent of their shots from the floor over the years. Why this high percentage year in and year out? The main reason for the high percentage is taking shots from within the shooter's range every time, not just sometimes. It should never be bombs away. Do your players know their ranges? What spot or spots do they shoot best from? A player should know his range and the area he should shoot from.

To be a great shooter, one must learn the importance of being on balance. Stress this point to your players over and over again. Every time one of your players takes an off-balance shot in practice or in a game, he should be reminded emphatically of the importance of being on balance.

Since this is not a book on the specifics of shooting, I will not dwell a great deal on this subject. But there are certain areas of shooting I feel should be mentioned. Balance is very important.

There are two other areas of fundamental importance to a shooter. One is that players should never take shots out of their ranges. What are their ranges? It might be a revelation to you to ask each of your players what is the point at which they cannot hit 50 percent of their jump shots. What are their best spots to shoot from on the floor? Every player has certain areas on the floor he shoots best from. Have you ever watched players on your team or another team warm up? In warm up players take shots from everywhere and anywhere. If they are this careless before a game, what do they do in their own shooting practice?

The other important shooting fundamental is concentration. Your players must practice concentration daily. We use drills, which will be diagrammed at the end of the chapter, to help each player improve his concentration.

Balance, range, and concentration, therefore, are three important ingredients to successful shooting. There are others to be sure, but these are the basics.

This leads us into the 3 play series for the shooting guard. We set our 3 man up on the right side because most teams are basically right-handed.

Pick and Roll

Our bread-and-butter option is probably the oldest play in the game. The pick and roll option is still one of the toughest plays to play defense against when it is run properly. The pick and roll is a staple play of most of the teams in the NBA.

Diagram 2-1 shows the basic alignment and indicates 1's entry pass to 3 and his cut. When we run the 3 play to the open side—that is, the side away from the stack—it is called the 34 play. This simply means the 3 play will be run to the 4 side. (See Diagram 2-2.) It is a quick 2 man game.

1 passes to 3 and rubs off 5, looking for a return pass. If 1 is not open, he stacks with 2 on the blocks. After receiving the pass from 1, 3 immediately shapes up, facing the basket in a triple threat position. As

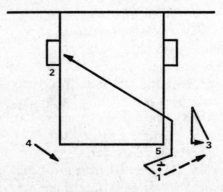

Diagram 2-1

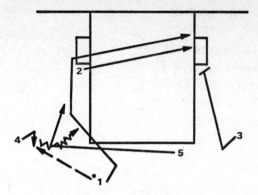

Diagram 2-2

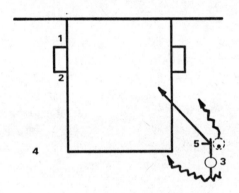

Diagram 2-3

soon as 1 rubs off 5, 5 sets a screen on 3's defensive man for a pick and roll move. (See Diagram 2-3.) 3 now has the option of driving off 5's screen to either the middle or the baseline, depending on how 3's defensive man is playing. As 3 rubs off the screen, 5 opens to the ball with his lead hand high to give a target for a pass from 3. 5 *must* roll the instant he feels contact by 3's defensive man. This is a brief moment when you have the defensive man beat. It is precisely this moment the offense must recognize and take advantage of.

Diagram 2-4 shows the 3 man driving the baseline. 5 opens to the ball with his lead hand up for a passing target for 3. 3 has a drive, a pass to 5, or a short baseline jumper.

In Diagram 2-5, 3's defensive man goes behind 5's screen, giving 3 the outside jumper. These basic moves are what 3 looks for first.

When 3 rubs off 5's screen, 4 knows he is to down screen with 2

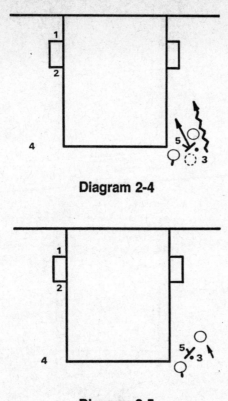

Diagram 2-4

Diagram 2-5

for 1 on the blocks. At this point we enter the basic pattern of the 3 play. (See Diagram 2-6.)

1 tucks and steps out for a possible pass from 3. As 1 receives the pass from 3, he should be on balance and ready to shoot. At this point 4 and 2 cross double screen for 5. (See Diagram 2-7.) It is important to note here that we like 5 to take the baseline route. 5 will be open at a better angle and positioned closer to the basket to shoot on this cut than he would be if he came over the top.

3 steps out for a return pass from 1 if 5 is not open coming off 4's and 2's double screen. 2 comes high for a rear screen for 3, while 4 continues to the wing area off the side of the ball. (See Diagram 2-8.)

At this point 1 has had several options available to him:

1. A short jumper from 8 to 12 feet

2. A drive to the basket

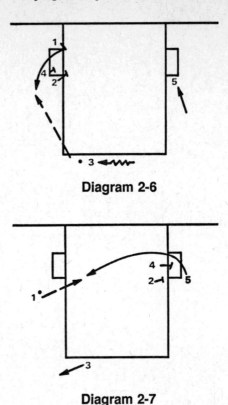

Diagram 2-6

Diagram 2-7

3. 5 coming across the lane off the double screen by 2 and 4

4. A return pass to 3 for a 15- to 17-foot jumper

5. A backdoor cut for a lob by 3 if the defense is applying pressure

6. A bypass to 4 at the wing

These are the high percentage options we are always looking for. What
is important here is for 1 to be able to read the defensive posture and,
as a quarterback would in football, take what the defense gives him.

   The drills presented at the conclusion of each chapter will help
you teach your players this vital aspect of the game. The better your
players can read the defense, the better your offense will be.

   In Diagram 2-9, 1 and 3 read the defensive posture and see that
3's defensive man is denying him the return pass. Seeing this, 3 sets

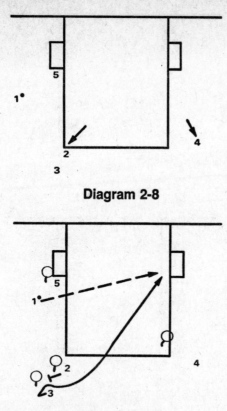

Diagram 2-8

Diagram 2-9

his man up for the rear screen of 2. When 1 sees he can't get the ball into 5, his peripheral vision should tell him of 3's defensive man's pressure position.

We know most teams will give help in this situation with 4's defensive man, thus taking the lob pass away. When this happens (see Diagram 2-10), 1, seeing the defensive coverage, knows 4 is open for the bypass. 1 has a natural passing lane open to him for the bypass, and 2 steps out at the free throw line. If this lane is not open, 1 can reverse the action to 2, who can now pass to 4. (See Diagram 2-11.)

Since 2 must follow post rules and not be stationary for more than two seconds, he down screens for 5 while 1 fills the point position. (See Diagram 2-12.) 4 now has the option of passing to 3, who is posted, or 5, who is flashing. To continue the basic pattern of the 3 play, reverse the ball on the top. When 1 has the ball and passes to 3,

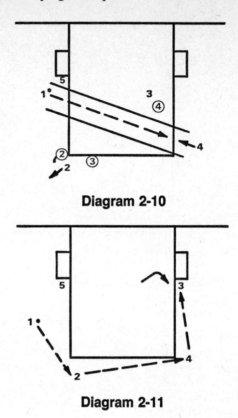

Diagram 2-10

Diagram 2-11

who is open on the top, the basic pattern continues. (See Diagram 2-13.) (Note: Diagram 2-9 shows the point in the action where this option first occurs.)

In Diagram 2-13, 3, after taking a pass from 1, passes to 4 and cuts for a quick give and go. If 3 is not open, he stacks on the blocks to the closed side. 2 down screens for 5, who flashes high. Remember that 3 has the option to drive the lane using 2's screen. (See Diagram 2-14.)

With the ball at the wing position in 4's hands, 5, who flashed high off 2's down screen, now sets a screen for 4. (See Diagram 2-15.)

As you can see, we now have the pick and roll with 4 driving off 5's screen. At the precise moment of contact by 4's defensive man, 5 rolls to the basket. As 4 reaches the edge of the lane, 1 down screens for 3 with 2 on the blocks. It is at this point that you run the basic

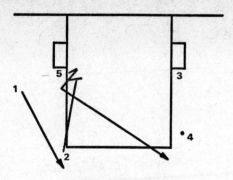

Diagram 2-12

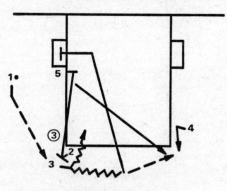

Diagram 2-13

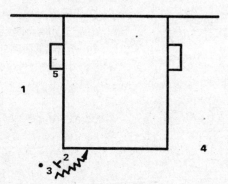

Diagram 2-14

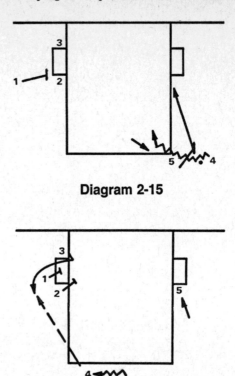

Diagram 2-15

Diagram 2-16

pattern a second time through. To continue the option, 4 should look to 3 coming off the double screen by 1 and 2. (See Diagram 2-16.) You now have your best shooter shaped up, on balance, and ready to shoot.

1 and 2 cross the double screen for 5 in Diagram 2-17. (See also Diagram 2-7.) How you develop and use the basic pattern of the 3 play is up to you. The basic pattern may be utilized in its entirety as a separate offense.

With the ball at the wing in 3's hands, you can continue the basic pattern of play as previously explained. (See Diagrams 2-9 through 2-13.)

34 Play

As mentioned at the beginning of the chapter, when the 3 play is run to the closed side it is called the 34 play. In our terminology, this

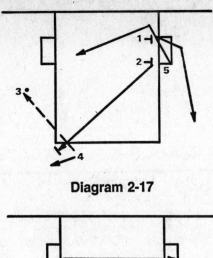

Diagram 2-17

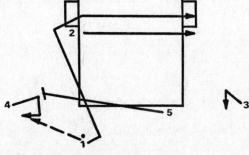

Diagram 2-18

simply means the 3 play to the 4 side. (See Diagram 2-18.)

Our 1 man passes to 4 and runs a give and go cut, looking for a return pass. The 2 man goes opposite to the stack, with 1 on the blocks. 5 crosses the lane to set a screen on 4's defensive man. 3 controls his man, ready to down screen for 1, with 2 on the blocks. (See Diagram 2-19.)

We are now in the same flow to the opposite side of the floor.

3 Drive

We use this variation of our regular 3 play when we are facing a team that believes in placing us under tremendous pressure at our point of entry into our offense at the wing position. Some teams apply extreme pressure at the offensive entry pass areas both ball-side and help-side. This brings a smile to our players' faces because they know

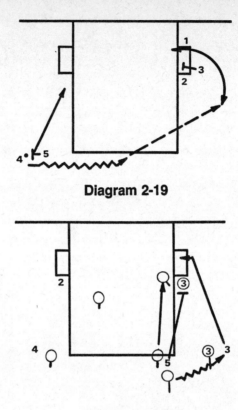

Diagram 2-19

Diagram 2-20

it's layup time, or at least it creates a wide-open eight- to ten-foot area in the middle of the lane.

You must understand the defensive philosophy behind this style of play. The objective of the defense is to take you out of your offense. They do not feel you can hurt them on the back-door move. Nor do they believe your offensive players can stand the physical pressure for an entire game. Once you understand this, you can neutralize it.

We have always felt that the easiest player to screen is the one in close proximity who is guarding another player. This used to occur only at the post position, either low or high. We took advantage of the opportunity the pressure defenses were giving us and developed the 3 drive. It has been highly successful against this type of pressure.

In Diagram 2-20, the basic option of the 3 drive is shown. Our point guard, 1, drives right at the 3 man. As this happens, 3 back doors on the line of 45° to the blocks and pauses. 5 heads straight down the

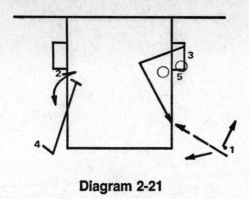

Diagram 2-21

lane to set a down screen on 3's defensive man. Because 3's defensive man is in a denial position, he is between 3 and 5 and in a position to be knocked off.

After 5 sets his screen, 3 rubs his defensive man off 5's hip and comes straight up the lane. (See Diagram 2-21.) As 5 sets his screen, 4 down screens for 2 on the help-side.

It is important that 3 read his defensive man's reaction to 5's screen. 1 must read the defensive posture of 5's and 3's defensive players. When 3 receives a pass, he must be on balance as he shapes up to the basket ready to shoot or feed inside to 5, 4, or 2. After passing to 3, 1 steps to the pocket for the return pass if his man helps out.

Diagrams 2-22 and 2-23 show what our players 1, 3, and 5 must react to as they read the defense. When 5's defensive man sees 3 is getting open, he will switch or jump out to help. On the switch by 5's defensive man, 5 is open as he posts up on this mismatch. 1 must read this as it happens and get the ball to 5. All 1 reads is where 3's defensive man is positioned on 5—behind, on the baseline, or high on fronting. (See Diagram 2-22.)

A smart defensive player, knowing he is going to get his head knocked off by 5's screen, will take a short cut and go over the top when he sees the screen coming. (See Diagram 2-23.) Seeing his man take the over-the-top route, 3 fakes behind and steps to the baseline pocket formed when his man is caught on the wrong side of 5's screen. 1 should read this defensive move and be ready to make his pass to 3 on the baseline pocket created by this defensive move.

Catching the pass on the baseline, 3 should be squared up, on

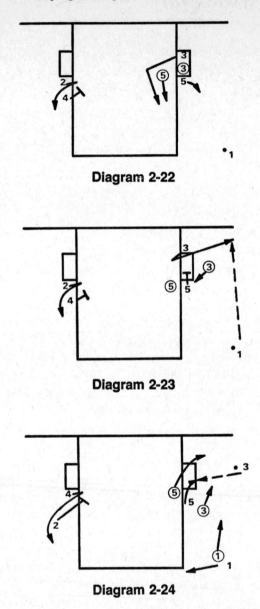

Diagram 2-22

Diagram 2-23

Diagram 2-24

balance, and ready to shoot. He does not have to put the ball on the floor. 5 posts up, looking for a pass from 3. (See Diagram 2-24.) 1 steps to the pocket for a possible return pass. 2 down screens for 4, who is on the blocks.

OFFENSIVE REBOUNDING AND
TRANSITION ASSIGNMENTS

All successful teams on offense face that moment of truth when the offense must convert to defense. This transition takes place either by the defense rebounding a missed shot or by a turnover. Each player must recognize this transition and convert from offense to defense. These moments are all too often when points are given away.

Since we are a man-to-man team defensively, each player is assigned a man to guard. In the confusion of transition, it can be very difficult for a player to locate his assigned man. Moments such as these are covered by one rule: Take the nearest man and apply as much pressure as possible. Slow the ball down, turn the man if possible, and, when safe, change to your assigned man.

You can lessen the danger of transition problems by using a combination of approaches:

1. Jam the rebounder to tie up the outlet pass.
2. Cut off the outlet receiving area.
3. Send additional men to the boards and get the rebound yourself.
4. Send all five players back quickly, each picking up the nearest man.

We advocate getting a high percentage of second and third shots through offensive rebounding. In the Inside Power Offense, rebounding is emphasized. The assigned offensive rebounding positions and transition defensive assignments will be diagrammed in depth.

Rebounding Positions

Diagram 2-25 shows the various positions we try to establish in our offensive rebounding plans.

The side of the court on which the ball is located is called the ball-side. The side away from the ball is referred to as the help-side. The position in front of the basket is referred to as the mid-point area. We rebound this position short and long.

Percentage Rebounding Theories

Playing the percentages in offensive rebounding is very important in the modern game of basketball. What is percentage rebounding?

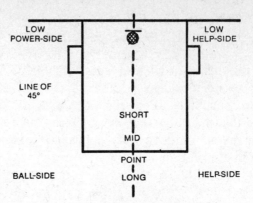

Diagram 2-25

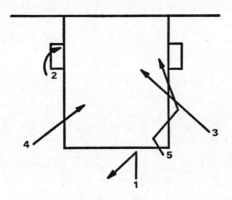

Diagram 2-26

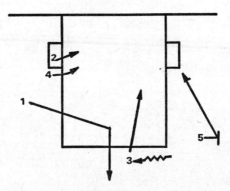

Diagram 2-27

Simply put, percentage rebounding is taking disciplined shots from an offensive position programmed to obtain the percentage shot, with excellent floor balance being maintained at all times. When taking this type of shot, your rebounders know where it will rebound to so they can be in the right spot at the right time.

Since most shots are taken from the side, the baseline area is the most critical rebound area. We teach our players to go to the baseline, using all the quickness at their command to beat their defensive men. Offensive rebounding is really just a matter of determination. The secret is in desiring to work for position by battling your defensive man every inch of the way.

The following diagrams will further illustrate our offensive rebounding and transition assignments for the basic 1-3-1 Inside Power Offense. The 5 or 2 man in the low post area fills the ball-side low area. The 5 or 2 man in the high post area rebounds opposite low on the help-side. Our 3 and 4 men rebound generally at the line of 45°. The 1 man can rebound the mid-point area short or long, but he must remember to be back deep since his main responsibility is deep safety. Diagram 2-26 shows these offensive rebounding assignments.

On a shot by 3 after he comes off 5's screen, the rebounding assignments are: 5 rebounds low ball-side, 2 rebounds low help-side, 4 rebounds on the angle of 45° help-side, 3 rebounds on the angle of 45° ball-side, and 1 rebounds at the mid-point or safety position. (See Diagram 2-27.) With 5 shooting, the assignments would be the same. 5 would be in the power area low, 2 would be help-side low, 4 would be help-side on the angle of 45°, 3 would be ball-side at the angle of 45°, and I would be at the mid-point. (See Diagram 2-28.)

Diagram 2-29 shows the assignments when 1 shoots the ball. 5 is the help-side low rebounder, 2 is the power ball-side rebounder, 4 is the ball-side rebounder on the angle of 45°, 3 is the help-side rebounder on the angle of 45°, and 1 is the rebounder at the mid-point and safety areas.

In Diagram 2-30, 2 takes the shot. 2 is in the power position, and 5 is help-side low. 4 will be rebounding at the angle of 45° on the ball-side, and 3 will be help-side at the angle of 45°. 1 will rebound at the mid-point area or be safety.

In Diagram 2-31, 4 takes the shot. Since 4 is taking the shot from

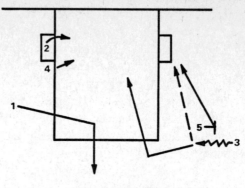

Diagram 2-28

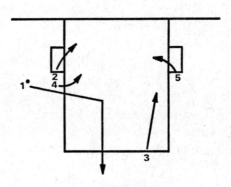

Diagram 2-29

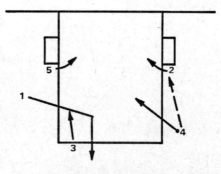

Diagram 2-30

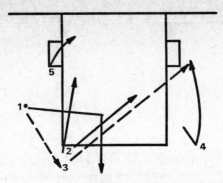

Diagram 2-31

the power area, he rebounds on the power side. 5 is in the help-side position low. When 2 is in the high post, he is responsible for rebounding opposite the 5 man at all times. With 4 in the power position, 2 rebounds at the line of 45° opposite 5. 3 rebounds on the line of 45° on the help-side. 1 is always at the mid-point or safety position.

The basic pattern of play of the Inside Power Offense can be incorporated as the entire offensive system against man-to-man defense or as the basis of a more complex system. When we first started, this was our basic attack out of a 2-2-1 set. With the advent of pressure, we evolved into our present set. Each year we have added to the basic offense, thus adding to the complexity of this system. The development of specific plays that fit the talents of your players is what this system is about.

Drill 2-1: Pick and Roll Move

Instructions: The 3 man starts with the ball at the normal wing position. 5 sets up at his normal position and comes across to set his screen. At first 3 must drive to the middle, while 5 rolls to the basket. Then 3 can drive the baseline, with 5 rolling to the basket. Later we add a defensive man to 3 and then add one to 5. At this point we also add our point guards, 1 men, to this drill. Rotate players after each successful play. On alternate days of practice, run this drill to the opposite side of the court.

Teaching Points: It is very important that 3 be squared up and ready to drive, shoot, or pass. 5 must roll to basket at the precise moment 3 rubs off his hip. We want his lead hand high to be a good target for 3's pass. It is important that 5 roll at the proper angle to set up the passer.

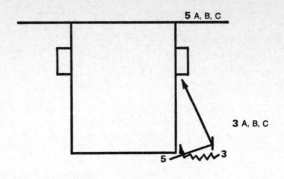

Drill 2-1

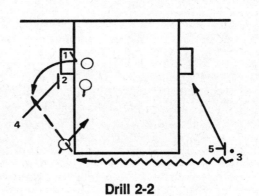

Drill 2-2

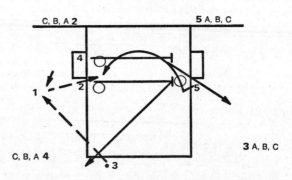

Drill 2-3

Time Sequence: We work eight minutes during the early part of the season. Later we cut this time to four and then two minutes.

Practice Pressure: When we add defensive men, 3 and 5 must beat their defensive men two out of three times. No mistakes are allowed or the defense wins. That means no violations or bad passes. 3 and 5 run if there are violations or bad passes, while the defense gets some water.

Drill 2-2: Screen Down on the Help-Side

Instructions: In this drill we have all five players involved, but we only use defensive players on 1, 2, and 4, adding one to each as we progress in the drill. 3 comes off 5's screen to the middle of the lane. 4 down screens with 2 for 1 on the blocks. 1 steps out for a pass from 3 and takes his shot. Rotate players as you desire. Offensive players rotate to defense. Defensive players rotate to the ends of their respective lines. On alternate days of practice, run the drill to the opposite side of the offense.

Teaching Points: It is important for 4 to time his move to when 3 reaches the edge of the free throw lane. At this time 4 down screens for 1 on the blocks. 4 should be reading 1's and 2's defensive players to determine where he sets his screen. 1 should jab step with a head and shoulder fake and rub off 4's screen. When 1 comes off the screen he should have his hands ready at chest level to receive a pass and be on balance and ready to shoot or pass. We want 1 to catch the pass from 3 as his inside foot touches the floor. This allows him to pivot quickly and face the basket without putting the ball on the floor.

Time Sequence: We work eight minutes early in the season. Later we reduce the time to four minutes.

Practice Pressure: If the defense forces a turnover or violation, they win. The offense must either score or attain a second attempt. Losers run.

Drill 2-3: Cross Double Screen

Instructions: We start this drill with the ball in 3's possession at the mid-point of the lane. 1 steps out from the double screen to receive the pass. 4 and 2 cross double screen for 5, who comes out on the baseline side to take a pass from 1. The defense is added to the 5 man first and then to the 4 and 2 men. Defensive players rotate to the end of their respective lines. Run this drill to the opposite sides on alternate days of practice.

Teaching Points: 1 must come out at the proper angle—the line of 45°—to receive the pass on balance and square up to the basket. 3 wants to use a bounce pass or a chest pass to hit 1 in his numbers. 5 fakes high and rubs off low, coming at an angle to the blocks with his hands high and ready to receive the pass. After catching the pass, 5 should pivot and use his inside power moves. 1 has to be taught to read the defensive postures on 5, 2, and 4. The defensive players will determine when to pass and to which players.

Time Sequence: We work ten minutes early in the season. We reduce this to five minutes in the middle of the season and three later in the season.

Practice Pressure: The offense must score every two out of three times and attain either a second or third attempt. If the defense forces any mistake, the offense runs. If the offense attains its goals, the defense runs.

Drill 2-4: Back-Door Lob to 3

Instructions: 1 has the ball, and a defensive man is playing tough on 3. 3 sets his man up for a back-door cut to the backside of the basket. 2 sets a rear screen for 3. Add a defensive man to 2 and then 1. Rotate after a successful attempt. Run the drill to the left side at the next practice session and alternate in this manner all season.

Teaching Points: 3 has to set his man up for a screen by 2. He should use head and shoulder fakes along with a change of pace and direction. 2 must set a tough screen. 1 has to be taught to lob pass to the backside of the basket, using the proper arch.

Time Sequence: We work six minutes early in the season. We reduce this time to two minutes in the middle and later parts of the season.

Practice Pressure: 3 has two seconds to get open and receive the pass from 1. When we place a defensive man on 1, 1 has two seconds to make the pass. If the defense forces a mistake or turnover, they win; the losers run.

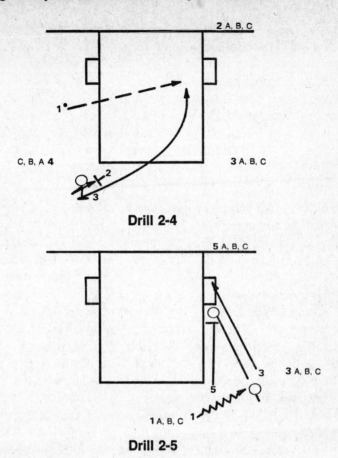

Drill 2-4

Drill 2-5

Drill 2-5: 3 Drive

Instructions: 1 drives at 3, who is being denied the entry pass. 3 cuts to the blocks and waits for 5's down screen. 1 passes to 3 as he comes up the lane. We start this drill with a defensive man on 3, add a player on 5, and then add one on 1. We alternate the side of the court the drill is run to each time it is used.

Teaching Points: 1 must drive hard and right at 3. 3 cuts hard to the blocks. 5 goes down the lane to screen 3's man. 3 reads his defensive man's position and either comes straight up the lane or steps out to the baseline pocket. Be sure 3 is always on balance and shapes up ready to shoot without putting the ball on the floor. As 1 drives hard at 3, he must read the defense and know whether

5 will be open or 3 will be open. Remember, if 1 has his man beat on this drive, he keeps going for a layup.

Time Sequence: We work eight minutes early in the season. We cut this time to four minutes in the middle of the season. Later in the season we cut the time to two minutes.

Practice Pressure: 1 and 3 must make the proper moves against whatever defensive posture is taken. If 1 and 3 make the wrong selection, they lose one point. If they lose three points, they run.

Drill 2-6: Spot Shooting with Pressure

Instructions: We pair two players to a ball. One rebounds for the other until he has completed shooting from all five spots. You specify what percentage of the shots he must make; for example, six out of ten from each spot. You set the standards. Where the pressure comes from is the percentage he must make *and* the time allowed—60 seconds at each spot. He must get ten shots off within 60 seconds and make whatever percentage you desire.

Teaching Points: The shooter must be on balance and have a quick release. Each player must catch the ball on balance.

Time Sequence: We work five minutes early in the season. Later we cut the time down to four minutes to speed up their reactions. Still later we cut the time to three and a half minutes.

Practice Pressure: For every spot at which they fail to reach the shooting goal for that day, they run. Sometimes we allow them to cancel out their minuses with their pluses, but not too often.

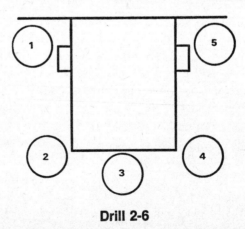

Drill 2-6

3

Coaching the Explosive Inside Game

1 Play Action Series

In today's offenses the point guard is concerned with running the offense, setting up the plays, and controlling the tempo. In other words, he is concerned with making things happen. The Inside Power Game Offense affords our point guard this opportunity. This is why we came to realize that our 1 man must be used to a greater extent. He must be a threat to the defensive posture and be able to keep the defense honest.

We did not intend our point guard to become our high scorer. What we wanted to do was hurt our opponent when he did score. This line of thinking developed as teams gave our 1 man the open shot when they were trying to defend against our Inside Power Game. It is in this situation that your 1 man can really hurt the defense. You can see your defensive opponents' faces as they look to the bench with a "What do we do now, coach?"

THE POST UP POWER MOVES

Whenever we have a 1 man who is taller than his defensive man or more physical, we like to run this option. The point man simply calls "1" to indicate what he wants to run. The 1 man passes to 3 and then jab steps to set his defensive man up for a rub off 5's screen. It is important that 1 learn to use his head and fake, change pace, and change direction moves. 1 then cuts to the blocks and posts up ready to receive the pass from 3. (See Diagram 3-1.)

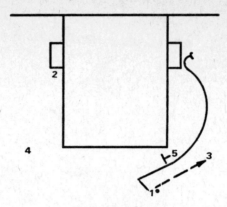

Diagram 3-1

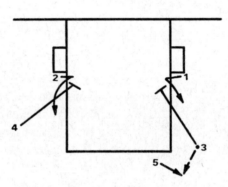

Diagram 3-2

In Diagram 3-2, 5 steps out to be a pass receiver for 3 if 1 isn't open when he posts up. As 3 makes a pass to 5, 4 down screens for 2. After making a pass to 5, 3 down screens for 1 on the blocks. 5 now has the option of passing to 1 or 2 coming off 4's and 3's screens. When 5 receives the pass he has to turn, face the basket, and read the defensive plays on his own man, 1, and 2, in that order. He must always be ready for his own opportunity to drive or shoot the 15-foot jumper. We like 5 to pass to 1 if 1 is open since he is your playmaker and should have the ball as often as possible. On 5's pass to 1, 5 goes opposite to down screen with 2 on 4's defensive man. (See Diagram 3-3.) 3 posts up on the blocks to receive a pass from 1. The 1 man now has the option to pass to 3, who is posted, or to 4 who is coming off 5's and 2's double screen. If 1 reverses the action and passes to 4 and 4

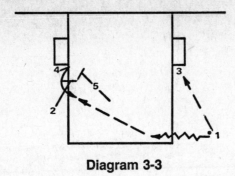

Diagram 3-3

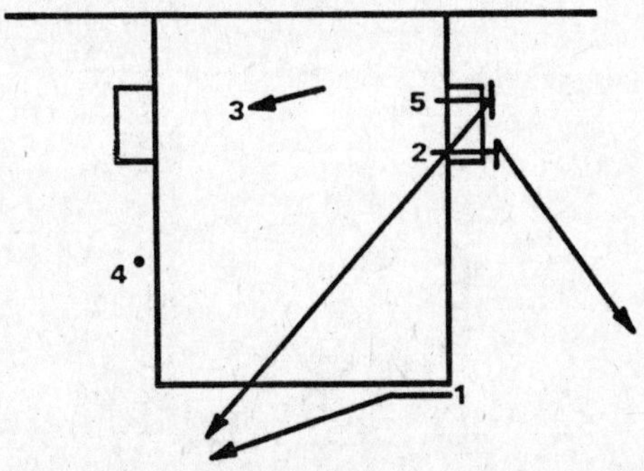

Diagram 3-4

doesn't have an open shot, our basic pattern of play as diagrammed in Chapter 1 is on. 5 and 2 cross double screen for 3, with 1 swinging on the top. (See Diagram 3-4.)

Note: The only difference in our basic pattern of play now is the exchange of 3 and 2 as our low post. As stated earlier, we like to post all of our players inside. Very few teams can defend against your guards and forwards from the low post area. Thus, we feel it is to our advantage to use this avenue of attack.

Diagrams 3-5, 3-6, 3-7, and 3-8 show the basic pattern of play as it would be run from the 1 play series. In Diagram 3-5, 1 is being overplayed by his defensive man. 4 should be reading this defensive posture, as should 1. 1 should back cut off 5's butt screen. 4 then lobs to the back side of the basket. When 1's defensive man is playing

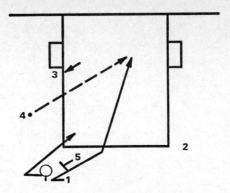

Diagram 3-5

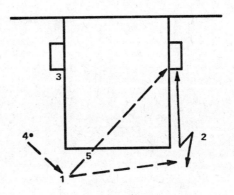

Diagram 3-6

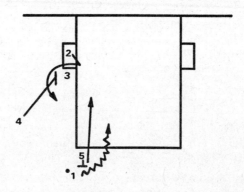

Diagram 3-7

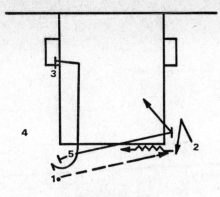

Diagram 3-8

normally, 4 can reverse the action to 1. (See Diagram 3-6.) 1 now looks for 2 to back door if overplayed or to step up to receive a pass from 1. When 2 does not receive a lob pass on his back-door cut, he crosses to the blocks opposite and stacks with 3. (See Diagram 3-7.) 5 now sets a butt screen for 1 to drive to the open side. 4 and 5 down screen with 3 for 2, who is on the blocks. 1 has a drive or pass to 2, who is coming off the triple screen by 5, 4, and 3.

When 1 sees 2's defensive man sagging off, he passes to 2, who is stepping out. The point guard can now continue the basic pattern from the 1 play series or change to a 3, 4, 5, or 2 play series. Diagram 3-8 shows 1 passing to 2 and changing to the 3 play series. With 1's pass to 2 and his cut opposite to stack with 3, 1 has indicated that the 3 play be run. After butt screening for 1, 5 screens for 2 in a pick and roll move.

OPEN SIDE CUT

Even though the 1 play is shown being run to the closed side here, it can also be run to the opposite side. We call this play the open side cut. All of our offensive series can be run to the opposite side. Diagram 3-9 shows the open side cut. The difference here is that 1 can try to beat his man with a quick cut in an open space minus a screen from 5, 2 clears opposite, and 1 posts up if he was not open on the give and go cut. Otherwise, the 1 play is run from this side the same as it was from the closed side. Remember, the high post, 5, indicates the open or closed side by where he sets up. (See Diagram 3-10.) The 1 play clear

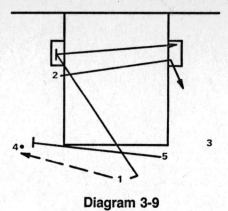

Diagram 3-9

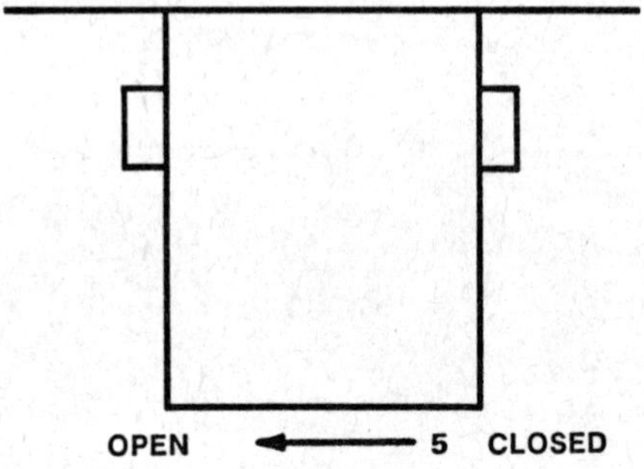

OPEN ← 5   CLOSED

Diagram 3-10

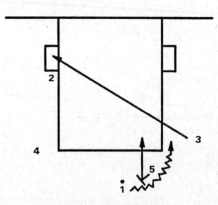

Diagram 3-11

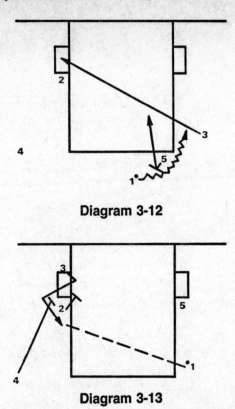

Diagram 3-12

Diagram 3-13

out can be run with the dribble entry (see Diagram 3-11) or clear with a pass entry. (See Diagram 3-12.) The point man may immediately take the jumper, drive to the right, or pass to 5, who is rolling to the basket. If none of these options is available, 1 looks to reverse the ball to 3, who is coming off a down screen by 4 and 2. (See Diagram 3-13.) From this point, the option is the same as diagrammed earlier in the chapter.

TRANSITION AND REBOUNDING ASSIGNMENTS

The rebounding assignments are the same as described in Chapter 1. Our 5 man goes opposite the low post to rebound help-side. 3 and 4 rebound at the angle of 45°, either ball-side or help-side. The point guard goes to the mid-point area and rebounds long or is defensive safety.

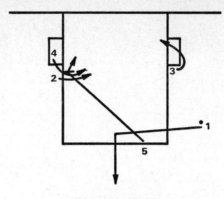

Diagram 3-14

Rebounding assignments are shown in Diagram 3-14. Since 3 was posted low and took the shot, he rebounds ball-side low. The high post, 5, who down screened, follows his rule and rebounds the blocks low on the help-side. 2 follows his rule and goes opposite the high post, but this time at the angle of 45° on the ball-side. 4 rebounds at the angle of 45° on the help-side. 1 goes to the mid-point or safety position.

The transition game starts the moment your team takes a shot. We consider offensive rebounding the first phase of the transition. The second phase begins the instant your team loses the rebound or scores a basket. The *conversion* from offense to defense is where many games are won or lost.

In the transition period our players have several responsibilities:

1. The point guard is to be as deep as their deepest man.

2. The nearest defender to the rebounder is to jam their rebounder. Make him pivot or put the ball on the floor.

3. All other players are to sprint to the nearest players ahead of them. In doing so, they must cross through the offensive passing lanes. They should never run with their backs to the ball.

Diagrams 3-15 and 3-16 illustrate what we are trying to accomplish in our transition from offense to defense. Diagram 3-16 shows what happens when 5 takes a shot from the free throw line in the 1 play series. *Note:* Since we are converting to defense, our offensive

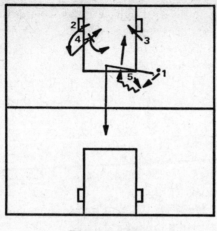

Diagram 3-15

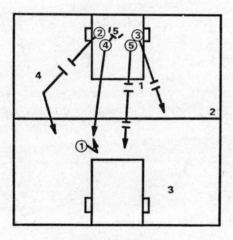

Diagram 3-16

players are shown in defensive circles—(1)—because they are now in transition. 4 jams the rebounder, number 5, and 2 sprints through the passing lane of the nearest man, opponent player number 4, looking to intercept the outlet pass. Player 3 does the same thing on his side to the nearest opposing player, receiver number 2. 5 sprints through the passing lane of number 1. After jamming the rebounder, 4 sprints to the free throw line area and looks for anyone flashing into the post area.

The transition from offense to defense is one of the most critical areas in the game today. The championship teams excel in this phase of the game. This is becoming more evident in basketball every year, which justifies the extra time a wise coach spends on this phase.

Drill 3-1: Pass to 3 or 4 Man

Instructions: The 1 man works on his pass to the 3 or 4 man. In this case, the 3 man will be used. We add a defensive man to the 1 man later in the drill.

Teaching Points: The 3 and 4 men must use proper footwork to get open against the the pressure defense. Make sure they use angle cuts, V cuts, and not circles. The 1 man must make the correct pass to the outside shoulder of the receiver. After receiving the pass, 3 must turn and face the basket. Add a second defensive man to the 1 man. This puts added pressure on the point guard. 1 must now free himself of defensive pressure and make a proper pass. Rotate players in as you direct.

Time Sequence: We work five minutes early in the season. Later we cut this time to three- and two-minute segments.

Practice Pressure: Allow two seconds for 3 to get open to receive the

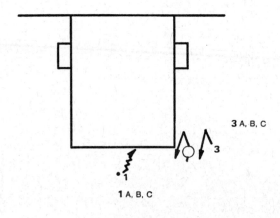

Drill 3-1

pass. When a defensive man is added to the 1 man, the 1 man has two seconds to complete the pass. The loser runs.

Drill 3-2: 1 Man Posting Up

Instructions: 1 passes to 3 and, using head and shoulder fakes with change of pace and direction moves, cuts off 5's butt screen. 1 now posts up on the blocks, ready to receive the pass from 3.

Teaching Points: It is important that 1 learn to use good fakes and sharp cuts to rub his man off 5's butt screen. 5 must set his screen with a wide base and make sure he is not moving. 3 shapes up and makes the pass to 1 in the low post. Add a defensive man to the 1 man and then to the 5 man. Rotate players from offense to defense and then to the end of the line.

Time Sequence: We work seven minutes early in the season. We cut this time to five minutes after the season opens and to two minutes later in season.

Practice Pressure: Allow two seconds for 3 to get open. 1 must get open on the blocks. If the defense wins, 1 and 3 run, but if the offense is successful, the defense runs, with the offense staying out on the floor. This practice pressure is used only when we have at least two defensive men in the drill.

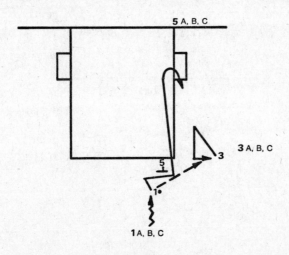

Drill 3-2

Drill 3-3: 5 Step Out and Down Screen

Instructions: 5 steps out to receive the pass from 3. After passing to 5, 3 down screens for 1. 1 rubs off to receive the pass from 5. 1 then looks to feed 3, who is posted up inside on the blocks. We start with no defense and then add one, two, and finally three men. Where you place each defender is up to you. For example, if you want to work on screening, put a defensive man on the 1 man. Move to the opposite side of the floor and work the 4 man.

Teaching Points: 5 must step out at the proper angle, with his receiving hand high. Make sure players get their bodies behind the ball as they catch passes. They must pivot and shape up to the basket ready to pass, drive, or shoot. Most important: the 5 man must read the defense as he shapes up to the basket. Did the defense switch? Is the 1 man open for a direct pass from the top before 3 down screens? Is 1 open, rubbing off 3's screen? 5 *must learn* to read the defensive postures on 1 and 3 instinctively. His close-up vision will tell him what his own defensive man is doing. 1 must set his man up and be sure to rub tight to 3's baseline hip. 1 must read the defensive posture of 3's man and his own.

Time Sequence: We work seven minutes early in the season. Later we cut this time to five-minute and then three-minute segments.

Practice Pressure: When you are using only one or two defensive men, allow two seconds for 1, 3, or 5 to get open. Losers run. With 3 defensive men, we change the pressure by having the

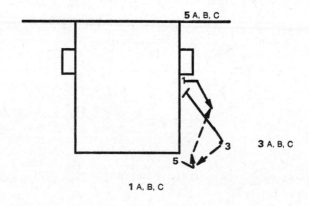

Drill 3-3

offense win if they can get the ball inside to 1 or 3 three straight times and score. If the defense forces a turnover, they fast break. The offense must convert to defense. If the defense converts successfully, the offense runs. Another method of producing practice pressure is to have the offense execute the option, reading the defensive positioning and making the selection. Of course, you will determine whether it is the correct choice. *Note:* When we are using this practice method, we stop play and have them analyze why they made the selection they made. If their choice is different from ours, we will explain our reasoning.

Drill 3-4: Down Screen Help-Side

Instructions: We are teaching 4 and 2 how to screen against the help-side posture in this drill. Start with one defensive man. When this option is run to the left side, 3 and 2 will screen against the help-side defense. Defend against the 2 man first and then add a defensive player to the 4 man. Later we will add a defensive player on the 5 man.

Teaching Point: It is important to emphasize the proper timing to 4 on this down screen move. 4 should be faking high and down screen as 5 receives the pass from 3. 4 must set the screen at the proper angle and be aware of the three-second violation. 2 must jab step

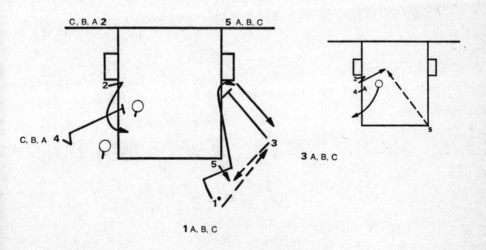

Drill 3-4

and head and shoulder fake to set his man up for the rub off 4. 2 has to read how his man is playing him. If 2's defensive man tries to beat him over the top, he should come back quick to the inside for an easy layup (see insert). If there is a switch by 2's and 4's defensive men, 4 should open up for a pass from 5.

Time Sequence: We work seven minutes early in the season. We later cut the time to four and then two minutes.

Practice Pressure: The offense must make a successful screen and get open two straight times and then three straight times. If the offense fails, they run. If the defense fails, they run. Later we insist that the offense score two or three straight times. Whenever there is a violation, such as a three-second violation, traveling, or an illegal screen, the offense either runs or the defense is awarded a point. Later in the season we use a point game in some of our drills. The point total could be any number you desire. For the sake of this explanation we will use five points. For the offense to win, they must score either three field goals or two field goals and one free throw or offensive rebound. The defense is awarded one point for each turnover, rebound, and offensive violation and two points for the completion of a transition game into a score. Losers run.

4

Adding the

Explosive Inside Power

Game 4 Play Series

To blend with our offensive thinking, the 4 man should be a good shooter with less range than the 3 man. We prefer him to be an effective shooter in the 12- to 15-foot range. If his range is greater, it is just like icing on the cake.

Our main consideration is his ability to perform in the areas of rebounding, defense, and jumping. You can substitute physical strength for jumping ability if you don't have a player who is a good jumper. You will notice later in the chapter why we look for a good leaper for this position and why a strong non-leaper will also do nicely here.

We have played players in this position from 5′10″ to 6′4″ in size. Size is not as important as what attributes this player has to contribute to the team concept of play.

BASIC OPTION OF THE 4 MAN

The purpose of this option is to apply pressure at a particular point in the defense. The 4 man is the player who applies this pressure. Our 1 man must then read the defensive posture to see how the defense is adjusting and what the adjustment is giving us. Often, defensive adjustments to stop this option have our 2 man open for easy shots close to the basket.

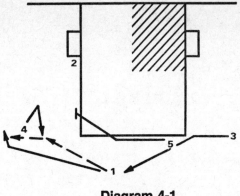

Diagram 4-1

Thompson Play

The point at which we wish to apply this pressure is close to the basket and the power area—the area all good offenses must attack to be successful. This is accomplished by an alley-oop pass made famous by David Thompson at North Carolina State.

In Diagram 4-1 our point guard, 1, passes to 4 and goes behind 4 for a return pass. This is the nonverbal key for signaling that the 4 play is on. 4 returns the pass to 1 as 5 crosses the lane to set a screen on the second hash mark. 3 swings up on top.

We have now cleared the backside of the defense and brought our best shooter, 3, to the top of the circle. The pressure point of our attack is to this open area opposite the 2 man—the shaded area. 4 returns the pass to 1, who shapes up to the basket. *Note:* We call this play 43 when we initiate this option to the 3 side of the floor.

After 4 returns the pass to 1, he rubs off 5's screen (see Diagram 4-2) to the blocks opposite, looking for the over-the-top pass from 1.

⸱ Our point guard, 1, must read the defense as it adjusts to take away this pass. The most obvious move is to drop off the defensive man on 3 to help out on 4. (See Diagram 4-3.) This move is fine with us since our best shooter will be left wide open at the free throw line. 1 should pass to 3, who is shaped up to receive the pass, on balance, and ready to shoot, pass, or drive.

When 4 sees he is not open for the Thompson pass and 1 has passed to 3, who is on the top, 4 posts up on the blocks. (See Diagram 4-4.) 3 can then pass to 4, who is posted up on the blocks, since his

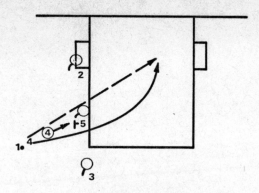

Diagram 4-2

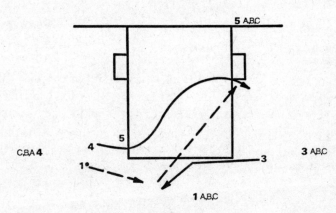

Diagram 4-3

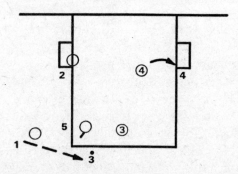

Diagram 4-4

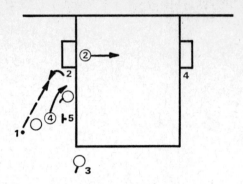

Diagram 4-5

man, in taking away the lob pass, cannot possibly recover to a position to prevent a quick pass from 3, who is on the top, down to 4, who is on the blocks.

If the defense decides this is not a successful move, they usually have the defensive man on 2 drop off to help out. (See Diagram 4-5.) When 1 sees this defensive adjustment, he passes to 2, who is posted up on the blocks, for a high percentage shot. This is where we really want the ball in the first place—in the hands of our low post, 2 man.

Most teams are reluctant to allow the offensive 3 man to receive a pass because of his shooting ability. They must try to get help elsewhere.

Helping out with 5's defensive man is another way to try to prevent the Thompson pass. Diagram 4-6 shows this defensive strategy. 5 can shoot a medium-range jumper or feed 2 or 4, who are on the blocks. If 5 chooses to shoot, we are in an excellent rebounding position. This is why we like our small forward to be a strong player if we do not have a real leaper in the 6' to 6'4" range at this position. He is the backside rebounder for a great number of shots taken by 2 and 5.

Some teams will try to double up upon 1 when he receives the pass from 4. (See Diagram 4-7.) When this happens, 4 simply slides to the baseline pocket to receive a return pass from 1. 4 and 2 are now in a two-on-one position. If 4 takes a perimeter shot, 5 rebounds backside. If 4 decides to drive, 2 clears to the opposite blocks. 2's defensive man has to choose which man to take. 4 either passes or shoots, depending on 2's defensive man's move. (See Diagram 4-8.)

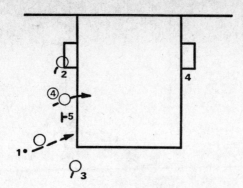

Diagram 4-6

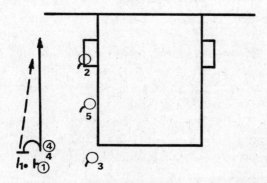

Diagram 4-7

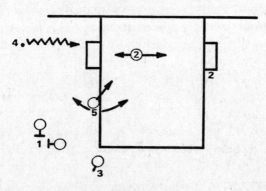

Diagram 4-8

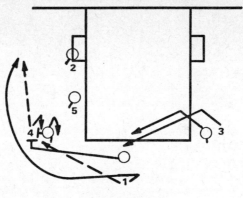

Diagram 4-9

When the defense tries to double up on 4, 1 continues to the corner pocket to receive a pass from 4. (See Diagram 4-9.) 1 and 2 must read the defense at this point and take what it is giving.

1 now has the same options available to him that 4 had. (See Diagrams 4-7 and 4-8.) He can take the perimeter 15-foot shot or drive baseline at 2 and react to 2's defensive man.

A variation of the Thompson option is to have 4 start to rub off 5's screen as usual but to pivot and open to the ball as he slides down the lane. 4 should always be alert to this move if his defensive man tries to beat him over the screen. (See Diagram 4-10.) 1 must read the defensive adjustment to this option and then get the ball into the open man, preferably in the power area.

The over-the-top pass is available to 1 as 2 goes opposite to the block. If 2's defensive man hesitates to help on 4, 1 should lob pass to 2. (See Diagram 4-11.) If 1 reverses the ball to 3, who is on the top, 3 can pass to 2, who is posted on the blocks. (See Diagram 4-12.) This would be the same as the regular 4 option, where 3 passes to 4. (See Diagram 4-4.)

The basic pattern of play can be initiated with the ball on top in 3's hands. If 3 chooses not to shoot or pass to 4 or 2, who are posted up on the blocks, he can initiate the continuity phase by passing to 4 or 2, whichever one happens to be posted, as they swing out to the 3 position. (See Diagram 4-13.)

At this point 3 cuts behind 4 for a return pass. 1 swings on top as 5 and 2 cross to the ball-side. (See Diagram 4-14.) With this movement

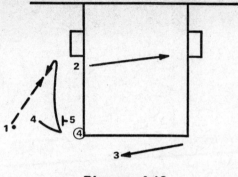

Diagram 4-10

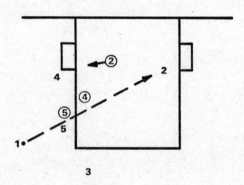

Diagram 4-11

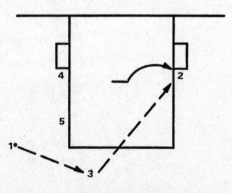

Diagram 4-12

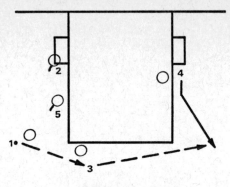

Diagram 4-13

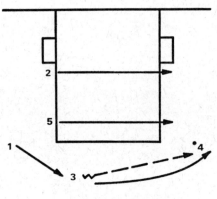

Diagram 4-14

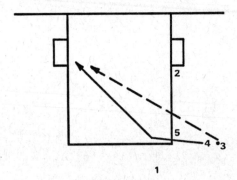

Diagram 4-15

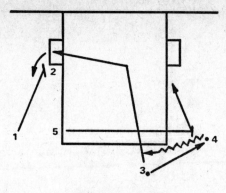

Diagram 4-16

we can run the 4 play from the opposite side of the floor. (See Diagram 4-15.)

This play can be repeated until you are able to obtain the high percentage shot you desire.

If 3 (see Diagram 4-13) chooses not to continue the basic pattern of the 4 play and decides to change to another option, such as the 3 play, he indicates the change by his cut or vocal command. (See Diagram 4-16.)

Of course, the play can be changed to the 1, 2, or 5 play if 3 chooses to. Since 3 called the 3 play, the action continues as described in Chapter 3 on the 3 play.

Back-Door Cut

This move is indicated whenever you are facing a team that likes to deny the pass to your wings, in this case your 4 man. This type of pressure is very vulnerable to the back-door cut.

We flash the 2 man for a direct pass from our 1 man. As 2 flashes, 4 takes his man higher, setting him up for the back-door cut. This is a bang-bang play. The instant 2 catches the ball, 4 plants his outside foot and cuts to the blocks with his lead hand out as a target for 2's bounce or lob pass. (See Diagram 4-17.) 2 now has the side cleared for his drive to the basket. (See Diagram 4-18.)

As 2 faces the basket to drive, 5 goes down the lane to set a pinch screen with 4. 3 knifes through as 5 and 4 close down and pinch off 3's

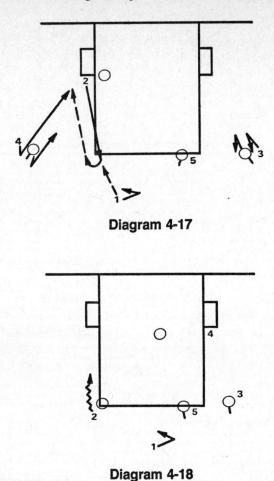

Diagram 4-17

Diagram 4-18

defensive man. If 2 cannot drive to the basket, he peels off to pass to 3, who is coming under the basket. (See Diagram 4-19.) 1 goes opposite and then swings back to be a receiver for a pass from 2.

On the return pass to point guard 1, 5 down screens for 4 and 3 comes off 2's screen. 1 looks to either 4 or 3 to see who is open. (See Diagram 4-20.) Either 3 or 4 looks into 5 or 2, who are posted inside. This is possible only if 1 holds his position; otherwise, 1 will indicate whether another option is to be run. (See Diagram 4-21.) But if 1, for example, goes behind 4 for a return pass, the 4 play is on. (See Diagram 4-22.)

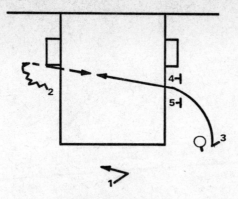

Diagram 4-19

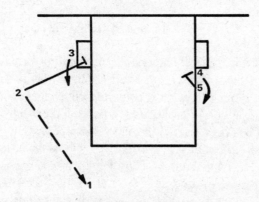

Diagram 4-20

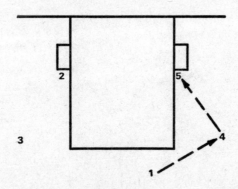

Diagram 4-21

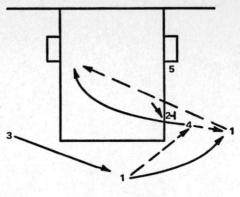

Diagram 4-22

REBOUNDING ASSIGNMENTS

As in the previous chapters, our rebounding principles are the same for each of our offensive play series. Our 4 play series, therefore, does not change our offensive rebounding concepts.

Let us look at our 4 play series at a point in the offensive pattern at which the ball has been passed inside to 2 and posted on the blocks by our point guard 1. (See Diagram 4-23.) If 2 shoots a baseline jumper, 5 rebounds at the baseline ball-side, 4 rebounds on the blocks opposite, 2 rebounds, at the line of 45° ball-side, and 3 rebounds at the line of 45° on the help-side. 1 goes to the mid-point or safety position.

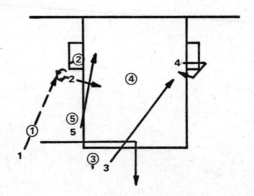

Diagram 4-23

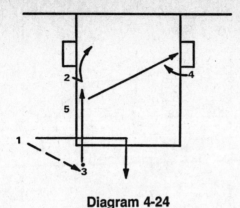

Diagram 4-24

With the ball on top and 3 taking the shot, the rebounding assignments are the normal assignments. 2 and 5 rebound on the blocks, with 4 and 3 rebounding at the line of 45°. 1 goes to the mid-point or safety position. (See Diagram 4-24.)

As you can see, we have the critical rebounding areas covered at all times. These high percentage areas must be covered to insure winning.

TRANSITION ASSIGNMENTS

The instant your opponent secures the defensive rebound, you are in the transition game. Remember, offensive rebounding is phase one of our transition game, and the actual transition to the defensive perimeter is the second phase.

Diagram 4-25 illustrates our rules of transition as discussed in Chapter 2. The numbered players in circles are our offensive players. They are shown as defensive players since we are now considering ourselves as being on defense.

4 is closest to the opposing rebounder, so he must contest the outlet pass. 1 heads up court to be as deep as their deepest player, number 2. 1 should shade to 2's passing lane to cut it off. 3 crosses through 4's passing lane as he heads to the mid-court area and the nearest receiver in this area. 2 crosses through 4's passing lane, goes on to the next deepest receiver, and then goes to the middle of the lane.

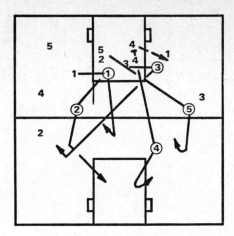

Diagram 4-25

After 4 jams his man, he runs a streak pattern to the blocks opposite the ball-side. Remember, this is the rule for any player who jams the rebounder. 5 is the off rebounder, so he crosses through the nearest mid-court area passing lane since we want to run through the passing lanes.

Whenever a player enters an open area—one with no more than one opposing player—his rule is to cross back through the passing lane and find the next nearest receiver while continuing down court.

Drill 4-1: Over-the-Top Pass

Instructions: The 1 man starts the drill by passing to the 4 man and going outside for a return pass. 1 receives the pass and shapes up to the basket (triple threat) looking at the defensive picture. 4 rubs off 5's screen looking for the over-the-top pass. 5 crosses the lane to set his screen as 1 passes to 4. Later we add defensive men to 1 and 4 and then to 5. This drill is rotated to the right side. It is then called the 43 play drill.

Teaching Points: It is very important for 1 to square up and be ready to pass, drive, or shoot. We want 1 to put a high arch on his pass and aim for spot just outside the neck of the rim on the backside. 1 does not aim for his receiver, player 4. 1 aims for a spot. We

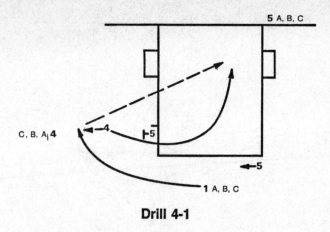

Drill 4-1

want to emphasize the height of the arch because it affords the added margin of error in case his aim is slightly off and is easier for 4 to catch.

Time Sequence: We work ten to eight minutes early in the season. As basic fundamentals, passing, catching, pivoting, screening, and cutting, have been mastered, we cut the time down to five minutes. For the last third of the season, the time varies from four to two minutes, but always with defensive pressure.

Practice Pressure: When the defense is added to 4 and 1, the offense must beat the defense two out of three times or run. The same rule is applied when we add defense to 5. Losers run.

Drill 4-2: Over-the-Top Pass—Read and React

Instructions: We start this drill either with the ball in 1's hands at the 4 position or by 1 passing to 4 and going behind 4 for the return pass. Which way we start depends on what aspect we are emphasizing that particular day. As 4 rubs off 5's screen, 1 reads the defensive posture of 2's, 3's, and 5's defensive men. Place defensive men on 4 and 2 and later add defensive men to 5 and the 1 man. The drill is then rotated to right side.

Teaching Points: 1 must be taught to look through the defense and read the position of each defensive player. Then he must react instantly to this defensive posture. 1 should be particularly alert to 2's defensive man. Is he loosing up to help out? If so, 2 should

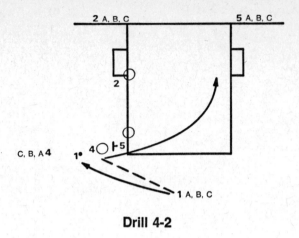

Drill 4-2

receive the pass—we like the bounce pass—from 1. What if 2's and 5's defensive men are fronting, low or high side? 1 must make the correct choice and use the proper pass. You are teaching the defensive picture to your point guard so his ability to react quickly improves.

Time Sequence: We work ten minutes early in the season. We cut to five minutes in midseason. In the last third of the season, time is cut to three minutes.

Practice Pressure: From the time 4 rubs off 5's screen, 1 has three seconds to decide who is open. 1 must make the correct choice 3 out of 4 times. If he doesn't, he runs. If the defense forces a mistake or miss by 2, 4, or 5, all four offensive players run. If the offense is successful three out of four times, the defense runs.

Drill 4-3: Reverse Action

Instructions: We start this drill with the ball in the hands of our 1 man at the 4 position. 4 rubs off 5 as 3 swings up on top. 1 reverses the ball to 3 on top. 3 passes to 4 posted up on the blocks and takes his jumper or drives to the basket, depending on what the defense gives him. As the drill is developed, we add defensive players to 4 and 3 and then to 5 and 1. The drill is then rotated to the right side. The offense rotates to defense, and the next offensive group moves in.

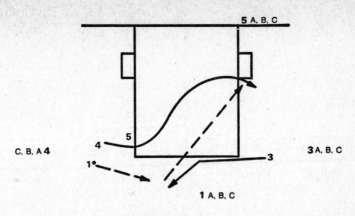

Drill 4-3

Teaching Points: It is very important for 3 to step out at a sharp angle and meet the pass. 3 must shape up to the basket and look inside immediately. He must read the defensive posture and get the ball inside to 4, who is posted up, if 4 is open. He must look for the drive or jumper if 4 isn't open.

Time Sequence: We work eight minutes early in the season. This time is later cut to five minutes and then three minutes.

Practice Pressure: 3 must make the correct choice in three seconds upon receiving the pass from 1. If he makes a wrong choice or there is a turnover, his unit runs. You decide if his choice is correct. If the defense allows a score, they run.

Drill 4-4: Double Team Trap on 4

Instructions: We always use defensive players on 1, 4, and 2. 5 is not used in this drill during early season work. He is added later in the season. 1 passes to 4, and as he comes outside for the return pass, 1's defensive man double teams 4 and the ball. 1 and 4 must recognize this defensive pressure and react properly. 1 slips to the corner pocket for a return pass from 4. He is now in a two-on-one position with 2 and his defensive man. The drill is rotated to the opposite side of floor. The offense rotates to defense when finished.

Teaching Points: It is very important that 1 recognize the trap and continue to the corner. He must square up to the basket and be on

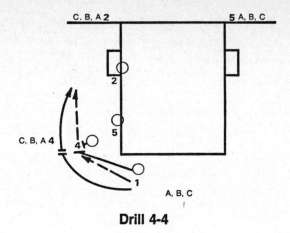

Drill 4-4

balance to shoot. 4 must use the proper pass—either a bounce or a lob pass. 4 must be sure to pass to 1, who receives the pass on balance and ready to shoot or drive. If 1 decides to drive, 2 clears to the block opposite. 1 must read 2's defensive man's move to decide whether to feed 2, take a power lay up, or make a baby jumper.

Time Sequence: We work five minutes early in the season. This time is cut to three minutes in the middle of the season.

Practice Pressure: The offensive players execute this drill five straight times. 4 must make four out of five passes correctly. 1 must be shaped up and on balance all five times. 1 and 2 must make the proper choice against 2's defensive man four out of five times. If the defense forces the offense into two mistakes, the offense runs. Otherwise, the defense runs.

Drill 4-5: Double Team Trap on 1

Instructions: 1 passes to 4 and goes outside for the return pass. At this juncture, 1 is double teamed by his and 4's man. 4 slides to the pocket, and 1 drops the pass off to 4. We reverse this drill to the opposite side with our 3 man. The offense rotates to defense, and the next group moves in.

Teaching Points: 4 must read the defensive posture and slide to the pocket shaped up, on balance, and ready to shoot, pass, or drive.

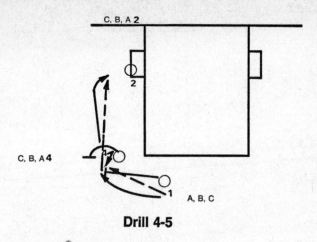

Drill 4-5

1 must read the defense and make the proper pass to 4, where he can catch the pass on balance. 4 then takes what the defense gives him—jumper, drive at 2, or pass to 2. If 4 drives, 2 must clear to the blocks opposite.

Time Sequence: We work five minutes early in the season. This time is cut to three minutes in the second half of the season.

Practice Pressure: The offense must run this drill five straight times, with only two mistakes allowed. The mistakes can be mental or physical. The 1 man is allowed no mental mistakes. The offensive group runs as many sprints as they made mistakes. If the defense fails to force two mistakes, they run.

Drill 4-6: L-Cut

Instructions: When 4's defensive man attempts to play this option by leaving early or by body checking 4's cut over the top, 4 uses an L-cut. In this drill we have 4 work on this move. When 2 sees 4 use the L-cut, 2 goes opposite to the blocks. 1 must learn to read defensive coverages and feed the open man. The drill is started with a defensive man on 4, 2, and 5. Later we add defense to 1. You can start the drill with 1 passing to 4 or at 4's position initially. The offense rotates to defense, and the defense rotates to the end of the line. Rotate the drill to 3 position.

Teaching Points: Players must learn to read and react. Correct any

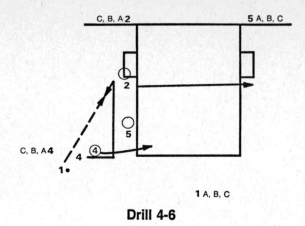

Drill 4-6

wrong response immediately. Explain why it was wrong and
show why. 4 must pivot on his inside (left) foot and open to the
ball with his lead hand high as a target for 1's pass. 4 should post
up if he has not received a pass by the time he reaches the blocks.
2 clears opposite and, depending on whether his defensive man is
helping out on 4, 1 can lob to 2.

Time Sequence: We work eight minutes early in the season. In midseason we cut the time to four minutes, and later we cut to two
minutes.

Practice Pressure: The offense must beat the defense three out of four
times. The winners get to choose the losers' penalty.

5

Expanding the Inside Power Game With the 5 Play Series

In our area of the country, the A.C.C. has had a great influence on the style of play used. Most prominent has been the University of Maryland under "Lefty" Driesell. The philosophy of getting the ball to your big men inside and letting them operate has proven successful for many teams in the A.C.C. and, in particular, Maryland.

When we developed the 5 play series, we used many of these same concepts. This series emphasizes the high post as a screener, passer, and shooter. However, since we believe in a point guard attack, we wanted to develop these ideas differently. Thus, the angles of attack, open-side and strong-side, were developed. To counter help-side defensive men, we added the post rotation clearout.

Since the success of the basic pattern depends upon their reacting together to defensive moves, it is important that these two men know each other's personal moves as well as possible. This calls for a great deal of practice in drill break-downs. All shots out of the basic pattern thus fulfill our demand for in-close shooting.

The 5 play is designed primarily for the high post (5 man). In this series the entry key by our point guard (1 man) dictates what option is to be run. *Note:* The 1 man has four ways to indicate what option is to be run:

1—Pass

2—Cut

3—Dribble

4—Call option by number

5 Play—Rule: The 5 and 2 men must never be standing still for longer than two seconds. This inactivity occurs if the 1 man is unable to make his entry into the offense. When this happens a lack of movement results, and what we want is movement at all times from all the players. We accomplish this by having the 5 man down screen for the 2 man, who is positioned on the blocks. (See Diagram 5-1.)

Our point man is taught to recognize the defense and to know what is the best option to beat it. His options were discussed in Chapter 2.

Direct Pass: The pass that keys this option is a *direct pass* from the point guard (1 man) to the 5 man. (See Diagram 5-2.) After passing, 1 clears in the opposite direction that 5 turns to. After catching the pass, the post man (5) reacts to the defensive pressure he sees and feels. He may pass to 3 as he back doors, shoot a jumper, or drive to the basket on 3's clearout. (See Diagram 5-3.)

The double screen option to the low post side can be run if the 5 man sees that this option is available. (See Diagram 5-4.) The 5 man dribbles to the side of the lane for a possible jumper or to set a double screen with the 2 man. As the pass from point man 1 went to 5 man, the 4 man cut to the blocks. He now steps out for a short jumper or a

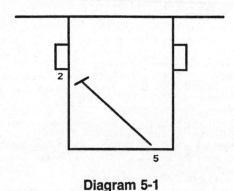

Diagram 5-1

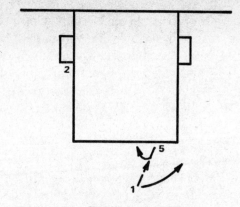

Diagram 5-2

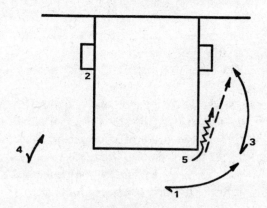

Diagram 5-3

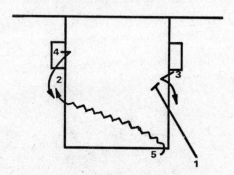

Diagram 5-4

drive to the basket off of a double screen. On the open side the 1 man has down screened for 3, who originally made a back door cut on the entry pass to the 5 man. The ability to execute the option properly is gained by repeated work on technique and reading the defensive posture. Our 5 man is taught to read the defensive variations through repeated drills. His abilities to react to defensive pressure should be instantaneous.

Exchange: This is called by the 1 man when he sees pressure being applied to the 3 and 4 players.

This option has been very successful against pressure defense when it is being applied to your wing positions (3 and 4 men). It is important here to note that 5 must be prepared to set his pick according to where 2's defensive man is. (See Diagrams 5-5 and 5-6.) *This move is designed to force a switch by the two defensive men involved.* If the switch is not made, 2 can drive to the hoop. (See Diagram 5-7.) If the defense switches to stop this offense move, 2 must be ready to pass to 5. 5 must seal his new defensive man on his hip, establishing good post position for 2's pass.

In Diagram 5-8, 2's defensive man on the exchange made a good defensive effort and fought over the screen. 2 can either drive to the open area or, as in this case, drive off 5's rear butt screen.

In Diagram 5-9, 2 has elected to drive to the open area. After 2 starts his drive, 5's defensive man switches off to help out. 5 rolls to the basket, looking for a pass and setting up a quick two-on-one position.

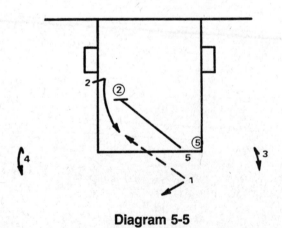

Diagram 5-5

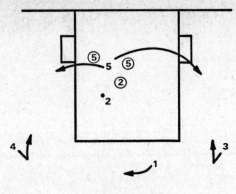

Diagram 5-6

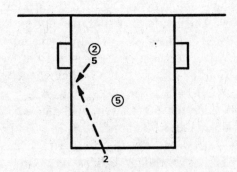

Diagram 5-7

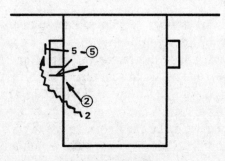

Diagram 5-8

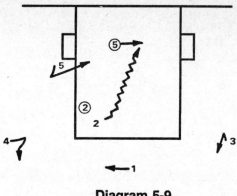

Diagram 5-9

At every step of this series, the defense will dictate our offensive option. For example, the man on 5 may fake a *jump in* switch and still guard 5. That is, defense number 5 comes out a step toward 2 and extends a hand, but he does not pick up 2. In this case 2 does not continue the drive, but takes a close-in short from the side.

The 2 man must be prepared for a back door cut by the 3 or 4 man. When the defense is trying to deny 3 or 4 the entry pass, the back door is available. The side the 5 man sets after his screen for 2 dictates whether 3 or 4 cuts. (See Diagram 5-10.)

Dribble 5—Post Rotation Clearout: The 1 man dribbles to a position at the foul line extended. 4 slides to the corner, 2 clears to the blocks opposite, and 5 rolls to the blocks ball-side. 3 rotates to head of the circle at the edge of the lane. (See Diagram 5-11.) When 1 puts the ball on the floor and drives at 4, 5 rolls to the blocks looking for pass.

Let's assume that the defensive man 5 has to be in one of the 4 positions shown. (See Diagram 5-12.) The defensive position that we are trying to force is to have 5 guarded one-on-one with no help-side defense.

The 1 man must read the defensive posture and make the correct pass. All post men must learn to seal their defensive men on their hips before receiving passes. This move will be detailed in the drill section of this chapter. As the 5 man takes advantage of the defensive weakness, our 1 man must make the correct pass. (See Diagram 5-13.) 1 sees defensive number 5 playing high-side. Number 5 seals and looks for a bounce pass lead.

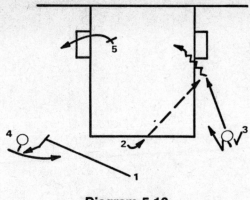

Diagram 5-10

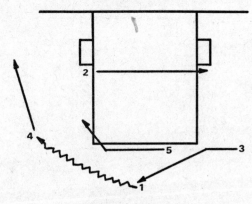

Diagram 5-11

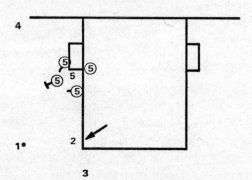

Diagram 5-12

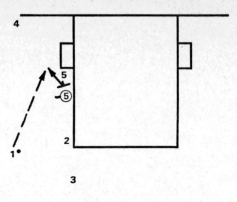

Diagram 5-13

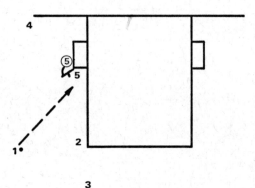

Diagram 5-14

In Diagrams 5-14 and 5-15 we show the various positions opposing defensive players have tried to stop this option with. Number 5 defensive man plays half low front side position. Number 5 seals and looks for the over-the-top or bounce pass.

In Diagram 5-15 the defense completely fronts our 5 man. 5 should seal his defensive man on his hip, with his target hand high. 1 reads this defensive posture and uses the over-the-top pass to 5.

Many factors, such as the defensive positions of our opponents or the offensive instincts of our players, determine when our patterns should be changed. This is illustrated when the defense gives help to the 4 man. (See Diagram 5-16.)

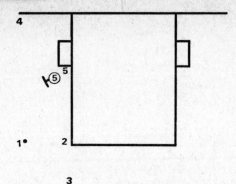

Diagram 5-15

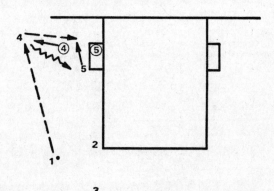

Diagram 5-16

When 1 sees number 4 drop off to help front 5, he should pass to 4 in the corner. 4 now has a 15-foot jumper, drive, or, depending on 4's defensive move, a quick pass into 5 for a power move. Since most teams will drop the defensive man off 1 after his pass to 4, 1 has the option to clear his man out. (See Diagram 5-17.) This is part of the basic pattern each play has built into it.

On 1's cut, 5 steps to screen on his defensive man. The 5 man then shapes up to receive the pass from the 4 man. (See Diagram 5-18.) Our post man 5 reacts to his defensive man's move to help out on 1's cut off his pick.

4 looks in to see the defensive posture on 5 and himself. They

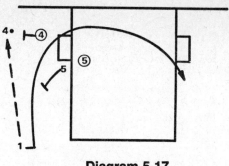

Diagram 5-17

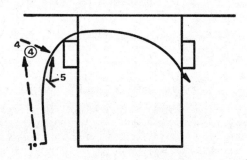

Diagram 5-18

must now react to what the defense is giving them. If 5 is not open, he rear screens 4's defensive man. 4 then drives off 5 for a pick and roll move. I should like to point out here, especially for the benefit of junior high school players and their coaches, that the dribble is offensive ammunition; it should be used for a definite purpose within the offensive pattern. As part of the basic pattern of play, 2 and 3 down screen for the 1 man on the blocks opposite. (See Diagram 5-19.)

Side Post Split: The 5 man indicates that this option is to be run by setting up in position on the first hash mark at the side of the lane. (See Diagram 5-20.) This is easy for our players to pick up since 5 always starts at the free throw lane. When he sets up initially at the side of the lane, 1 knows that the side post split is on. Our point man passes to 3 and screens 3's man. (See Diagram 5-21.)

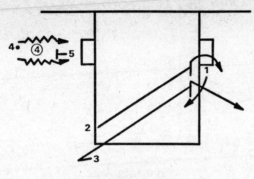

Diagram 5-19

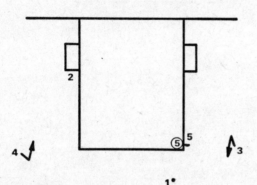

Diagram 5-20

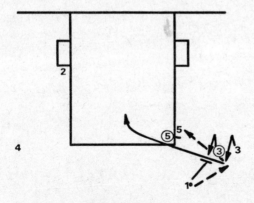

Diagram 5-21

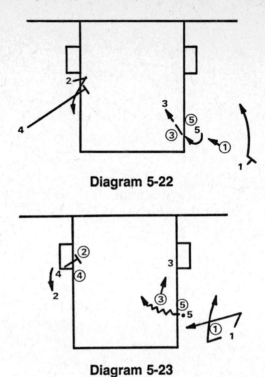

Diagram 5-22

Diagram 5-23

3 looks to 5. If 5 is open, 3 passes to 5 and cuts for the basket behind 1's screen and off 5's hip. *Note:* Our rule on all splits is that the man who passes into the post is always the first cutter. Players are cutters, screeners, and cutters, in that order. 5 should let 3 cut past him before turning and passing to him. This is the area he will break open in. As 5 receives the pass, 4 down screens for the 2 man. (See Diagram 5-22.)

In Diagram 5-23, 5 drives to the open area in the middle of the lane. He may have a short jumper or a layup or pass off to 2, who came off 4's downscreen, or to 3 when his man helps out. 1 should step to the open pocket, prepared to shoot if 5 passes him the ball.

If 3 isn't open, he steps to the blocks and comes off 1's screen, looking for pass. (See Diagram 5-24.) After the pass, 5 downscreens opposite, with the 2 man on 4's defensive man. (See Diagram 5-25.)

The 3 man should have an open shot. If not, he should look inside

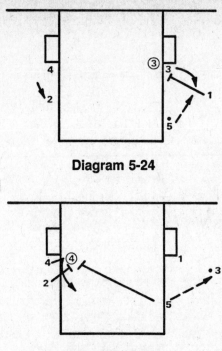

Diagram 5-24

Diagram 5-25

to the 1 man, who is posting up, or to 4, who is coming off the double screen by 5 and 2. The basic pattern of offense can be run at this point.

Although we very rarely need to run the basic pattern as a specific series, we can if the situation warrants it. To be effective, a variable play offense must consist of several distinctive series that are interchangeable. When a change is made from one series to another, however, no complicated moving or shifting of positions should be involved. You must remember that these changes occur in the heat of a ball game, and this is not quite the same as making them on the blackboard. Thus, just as the defense begins to sense the moves of one series, we quickly confront our opponents with a whole new set of passes, cuts, and shots.

It should be obvious by now that our offensive power is concentrated on the high percentage area close to the basket. Every series is designed to obtain the high percentage shot. In short, our wants are simple. Satisfying them, however, requires the same qualities of timing and discipline that characterize our entire system.

REBOUNDING ASSIGNMENTS

Our rebounding principles are the same for all five of our offensive play series. Therefore, the rebounding principles for the 5 play series are the same as the offensive rebounding rules for the other series.

Diagram 5-26 shows the rebounding assignments when 5 shoots from the blocks. 5 rebounds ball-side on the blocks. 2 is responsible for rebounding the blocks opposite. 3, who had rotated on top, follows his rule and rebounds on the line of 45° help-side. 4 rebounds the line of 45° ball-side. 1 has the responsibility of rebounding the mid-point or safety areas.

Anticipation of a teammate's shot is vital to offensive rebounding. This affords each player the opportunity to obtain that vital extra step to get inside his defensive man. When each player knows where (range) his teammate will shoot from and what type of shot he will shoot, he can improve his efficiency as an offensive rebounder. Diagram 5-27 shows our rebounding rules applied to another situation in the 5 series.

If 4 takes the shot from the corner, the rebounding assignments remain the same. 5 rebounds ball-side, and 2 rebounds help-side on the

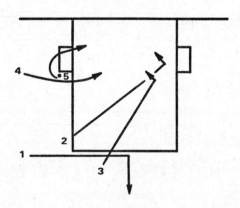

Diagram 5-26

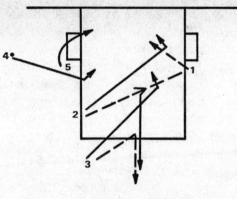

Diagram 5-27

blocks. 4 and 3 rebound ball-side and help-side, respectively, on the line of 45°. 1 goes to the mid-point or deep safety.

There is one adjustment we sometimes make when 1 is caught in a rebound position on the blocks. When we believe our 1 man is a better rebounder than the man guarding him, we let 1 rebound inside. The player rotated on top, in this case 3, takes the mid-point or deep safety position. The post man at the high post position, in this case 2, goes to the line of 45° help-side to rebound.

TRANSITION ASSIGNMENTS

Remember that once you have taken a shot you are in the twilight zone between offense to defense. You must go hard for those second and third shots, but once your opponent secures the defensive rebound you are in the transition game.

This twilight zone is phase one of the transition game. The actual transition to your defensive perimeter is phase two. The defensive perimeter is determined by where you decide to pick up defensively. Whether you pick up at full court, three-quarter court, or half court is determined by you.

Diagram 5-28 illustrates our rules of transition as discussed in previous chapters. The numbered players in circles are our offensive players; they are shown as defensive players since we are now considering ourselves as being on defense.

In this sequence in our 5 series, we have decided to keep 1 in as the backside rebounder. There could be several reasons, but we'll say our scouting report indicated that our 1 man could out rebound their player and we adjusted to take advantage of this situation. For this game, anytime 1 is in this position as a shot is being taken he stays and rebounds. He jams his man to delay the outlet pass and then runs a streak pattern to the blocks opposite ball-side; this is the rule for whoever jams the rebounder. 5 is the off rebounder, so he crosses through the nearest mid-court passing lane since we want to run through the passing lanes. Since 3 is the player on top, he assumes 1's responsibilities. 3 heads up court to be as deep as their deepest player, who is number 2. 4 rebounds help-side at the line of 45° and crosses through 1's outlet lane, hesitates and runs to the next deepest receiver and then to the middle of the lane. 2 crosses 1's passing lane, heading to the deepest receiver opposite the rebounder. 2 then heads to the foul line area, picking up the nearest open man.

Whenever a player enters an open man area—one with no opposing player—his rule is to cross back through the next passing lane and find the next nearest open receiver while continuing down court.

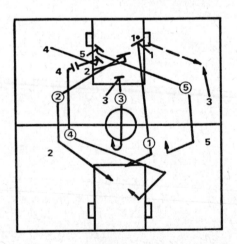

Diagram 5-28

PRACTICE DRILLS FOR OUR
INSIDE POWER 5 PLAY SERIES

Our practice drills are designed to condition our players to the type of game we play. In practice we develop the reactions that make our players respond automatically to each situation that arises. We practice with great intensity in each and every drill.

Drill 5-1: Direct Pass to 5 Man

Instructions: The 1 man passes into 5 against defensive pressure. The defensive man will give the 1 man different looks. We add a defensive man on the 1 man later to simulate a game.

Teaching Points: 1 man must learn to read defensive positioning by 5's defensive man. Is he playing half a man to one side, directly behind, or to other side? The 5 man must seal his man on his hip and extend his opposite hand to receive the pass. Stress the importance of his stepping to meet the pass. After catching the pass, 5 turns, faces the basket, and makes his offensive move. The point guard must use the correct pass to the correct pass receiving

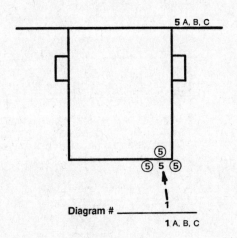

Diagram #

Drill 5-1

area. Add a second defensive player. Now 1 must work under added pressure. He should work on moving to the pocket if his man sags. He shapes up to receive the pass and shoots or feeds. New players rotate in as you direct.

Time Sequence: We work ten minutes early in the season. Later we cut the time to five minutes and then to three minutes.

Practice Pressure: Allow the 5 man two seconds to get open to receive the pass. Add a defensive man to the 1 man and give him two seconds to make the pass. The winner may have a drink of water. The loser runs.

Drill 5-2: Back-Door Cut

Instructions: The point guard makes an entry pass to 5 and steps to the pocket opposite 5's turn. 5 faces the basket and passes to 3 on the backdoor cut. We add defensive men on 3 and 1 men later.

Teaching Points: The point guard reads the defensive position on 5 before the pass is made. As 5 turns and faces the basket, he should turn opposite the defensive pressure. The 3 man works on taking his man high and setting him up for the back-door cut. His angle should take him to the blocks. 5 must make a proper lead pass for 3, who is cutting. We like to use the bounce pass.

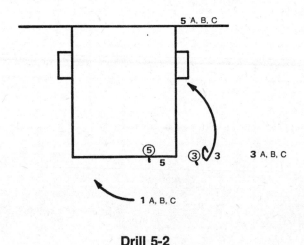

Drill 5-2

Time Sequence: We work five minutes early in the season. This time is shortened to four, three, and two minutes later in season.

Practice Pressure: Allow first the 5 man, then the 3 man, and then all three players only two seconds to get open. If the defense wins, the offensive player who miscued is penalized.

Drill 5-3: Down Screen Exchange

Instructions: 5 down screens for 2. The 2 man comes off 5's screen. The point guard makes a pass to 2. Add defensive men to 5 and 1 men as players improve on screening technique.

Teaching Points: Players must use the proper angle to set the pick, and 2 must come off the pick correctly. 2 must set his man up with jab step. If 2's defensive man attempts to beat the screen over the top, 2 cuts backside. 5 must be conscious of the three-second rule.

Time Sequence: We work ten minutes early in the pre-season. Later we cut the time to five minutes and then to three minutes.

Practice Pressure: Players work against time, generally two seconds. The pressure becomes greater for the offense as you add defensive players. The defense runs the transition game when it is securing the rebound. The offensive players must convert quickly to defense. The losers run, and the winners rest.

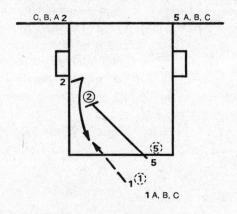

Drill 5-3

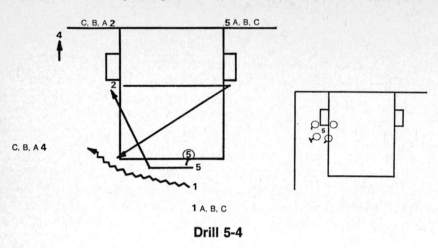

Drill 5-4

Drill 5-4: 5 Roll to Blocks

Instructions: The 1 man dribbles to the left or right. This move keys 5's roll to the blocks. The 2 man goes to the blocks opposite 5. Our point guard makes a pass to the 5 man in low post. Add defensive players to the 2 and 1 men as your players increase their skills. Later we add the 4 man and his defensive player.

Teaching Points: The ability of 1 to read and react to the defensive posture of 5's man is the key (see insert). The 2 man opposite reads his man and stays or comes to the pocket. The 1 man makes an over-the-top pass if 5 is fronted or a direct pass if 5 is played to the rear or the side. 1 must read what 2's defensive man is doing.

Time Sequence: We work five to ten minutes early in the season. As defensive players are added, we increase the time to ten minutes. Later in season the time is cut back to five minutes.

Practice Pressure: Two seconds are allowed for each phase of the drill once 5, 2, or 1 is in a new position. When there are three or four defensive men, the transition game is added. The winners get a drink of water.

Drill 5-5: Pick and Roll

Instructions: Start with the 1 defensive man on either the 4 man or the 5 man. Then add men until you have defensive men on 1, 4, and

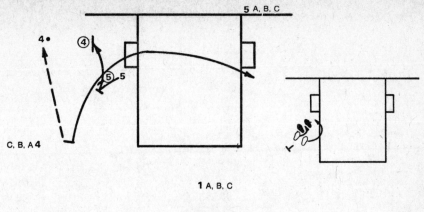

Drill 5-5

5. The point guard passes to 4 and makes his cut. The 5 man rear screens for 1 and then opens up for a pass from 4. If 4 isn't able to make a pass to 5, 5 rear screens 4 for a pick and roll move.

Teaching Points: 4 must be able to read and react to the defense on 5. 5 must be able to react to 4's man. 5 must use the proper foot work in screening, opening to the ball, and setting the pick for 4. He should pivot off of his outside foot to open up (see insert).

Time Sequence: We work seven minutes in early season work. Later we reduce this to three minutes.

Practice Pressure: We allow three seconds to get open and either make a pass or receive a pass. If the offense wins, the defense runs, and vice versa.

Drill 5-6: Split the Post

Instructions: 5 sets up in a side post position as 3 passes to 5. The point guard screens for 3 after the pass is made to 5. Defense is added to the drill as players' skills improve.

Teaching Points: The ability of 5 to position his body and seal the defensive man on his hip is most important. 3's ability to read the proper passing lane and make the correct pass must be stressed repeatedly. 1's correct screening angle and timing while 3 sets his man up for the screen is very important.

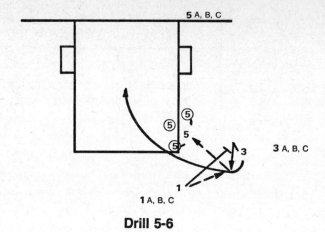

Drill 5-6

Time Sequence: We work ten minutes early in the season and five minutes later in the season.

Practice Pressure: When all defensive players have been added, we work on the transition game. We allow two seconds in this drill for 5 and 3 to be open and make the pass. The losers run, and the winners rest.

6

Running the

Explosive Inside Power

Game 2 Play Series

This series is developed around our 2 man and what he can do. Our 2 man always sets up in the very high percentage shooting area on the blocks. In addition, we feel that a player who has to fight one-on-one to get off a shot has less chance of scoring than a player who is coming off a screen or shooting behind one. Consequently, each of our offensive series is planned to give the potential scorer a chance to get off a shot without forcing it.

TYPE OF PLAYER

The type of player we generally find at the high school level is strong, ranges from 6' to 6'2", and has limited skills but is a physical player. He will give you all-out hustle and hit the boards with a relaxed abandon. His shooting range is generally limited to close to the basket—four feet to eight feet at best. This player is ideal for the 2 spot in our offense.

As you have seen in previous chapters, we keep 2 on the blocks most of the time. Options in each series help us to isolate 2 on the blocks. This series is not the only method used to get the ball inside to 2.

Our second Maryland State Championship team utilized a 6′ player in the 2 position; our first Maryland State Championship team had a 6′4″ player. The important point to remember is to play to the strengths of your players. Our 2 play series has added flexibility to take advantage of 2's abilities.

1 GUARD CROSS SCREEN

Diagram 6-1 shows the initial move to key the 2 play with movement keys. You may want to strengthen the key verbally. After passing to 3, 1 cuts behind 5's pick, setting a screen for 2, who is coming across the lane, and rubbing his man off 1's hip.

There are several important teaching points to remember. 1 has to locate 2's defensive man and set a firm screen. If 2's defensive man is high, 1 should set up higher. The reverse is true if the defensive man on 2 is playing low. 1 also has to be aware of the three-second rule as he sets his screen. This should not be a factor later as timing is perfected in your offensive team work.

2 must be taught to set his defensive man up for the screen. This is where movement without the ball is so important. 2 must perfect his head and shoulder fakes and his change of pace and change of direction moves. At the conclusion of this chapter, the breakdown drills will detail these important points.

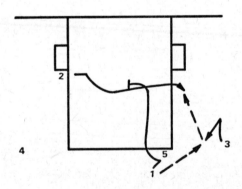

Diagram 6-1

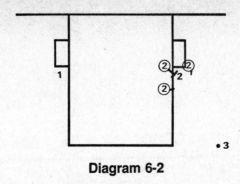

Diagram 6-2

As 2 comes off 1's screen, he wants to be on balance and ready to receive the pass from 3. We want 2 to have his target hand up to help 3 on his pass. After receiving the pass, 2 makes his offensive move according to where his defensive man is playing him. Is he high, low, tight, loose, quick, slow, or some combination of these? (See Diagram 6-2.)

3 must read 2's defensive man's move or position on 2 and make the correct pass to 2 so he can receive the pass on balance. Many coaches make a critical coaching error at this point. I can't emphasize enough the importance of 3's pass being made to a proper spot for 2 to be able to catch it on balance and ready to shoot. As a coach you are making one of the biggest mistakes when you fail to teach your players to make the pass to another player so he can handle it properly. How many times do you witness your (or opponent) players leaping or reaching to catch a pass? What happens? The timing is destroyed, and the defense is allowed that valuable split second to recover. Your player, who thought he was open, now forces up a bad percentage shot.

We continue our 2 play in Diagram 6-3. If 3 is not able to make his pass inside to 2, he looks to 4, who is rotating out on top. 5 crossed the lane after 1 made his cut off 5's screen and now sets a butt screen for 4 to rub off. 1 swings up to replace 4 at the wing position. Diagram 6-4 shows the basic pattern of the 2 play series. After setting a butt screen for 4, 5 crosses back to set a butt screen for 3. 4 reverses the ball to 1, who looks inside to 3, who is running a shuffle cut off 5's butt screen. If 3 is open, 1 passes inside to 3.

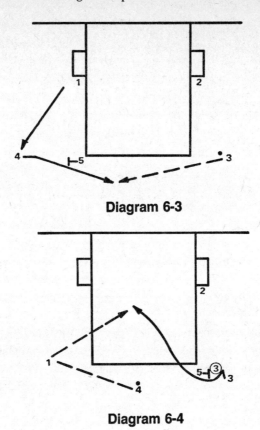

Diagram 6-3

Diagram 6-4

To digress a moment, we like to skip pass when the defense affords us this opportunity. Diagram 6-5 explains this situation. With the ball in 3's possession, 4, who is rotating up, is denied the pass by his defensive man. Seeing this, 3 looks to 5, who is crossing back over to set a screen for 3. 3 passes to 5, who immediately shapes up to the basket and looks inside.

Player 5 in Diagram 6-6 looks for 1 on the back-door move or 2 reversing off 1's cross screen. When 1 sees the skip pass to 5, he automatically reads and reacts, knowing he is to back door first and then screen for 2 on a reversal. 5 reads the defense to see who is open.

5 also has the option of driving the lane to either open area. (See Diagram 6-7.) This is an adjustment we have made for a defensive denial of a ball reversal to 4. But what happens when the defense also

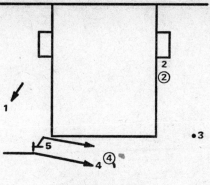

Diagram 6-5

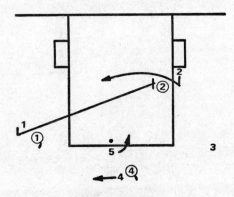

Diagram 6-6

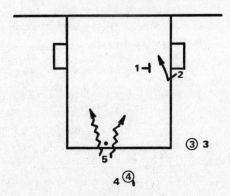

Diagram 6-7

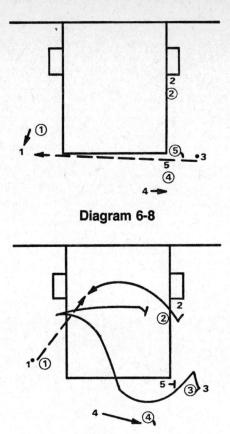

Diagram 6-8

Diagram 6-9

does a super defensive job of denying 5 the skip pass? 3 then looks to skip two passes and pass to 1, who is usually open, rotating up. (See Diagram 6-8.) We would now be back to where 1 had the ball originally as shown in Diagram 6-4.

The 2 play series continues from this point. (See Diagram 6-9.) 1 looks to pass inside to 3, who is coming off his shuffle cut. Seeing he is not getting open, 3 reverses to cross screen for 2 on the blocks.

At this point in the 2 series, we could change to any of the other series as the ball is either passed to 4 on top or 1 brings it out himself with the dribble. (See Diagram 6-10.) Whether 1 passes or dribbles out to 4 depends on whether your 4 man is a good passer and ball handler. Let's say we use the dribble move here most of the time.

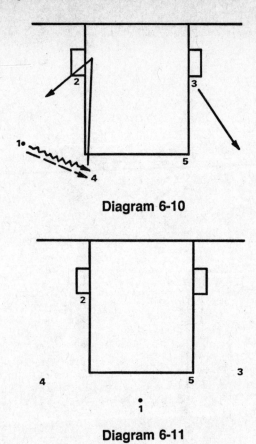

Diagram 6-10

Diagram 6-11

With the ball on top in 1's hands, you can see we are now in our original positions. (See Diagram 6-11.) From this offensive set, 1 can run any option he feels the defense is giving us.

EXPLOSIVE INSIDE
REVERSE ACTION DOUBLE SCREEN

When 2 is a good medium-range jumper, we like to use this option in our 2 play series. (See Diagram 6-12.) 4 downscreens for 2 on the blocks. 2 rubs off 4's screen while coming out to the line of 45°. 2 should be on balance and in position to receive the pass from 1. Upon catching 1's pass, 2 should be ready to shoot, provided he received the

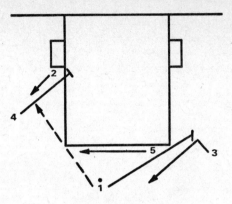

Diagram 6-12

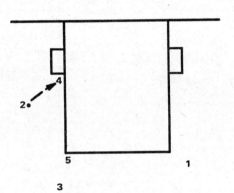

Diagram 6-13

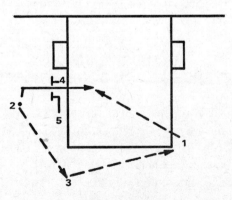

Diagram 6-14

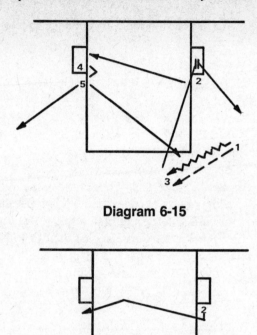

Diagram 6-15

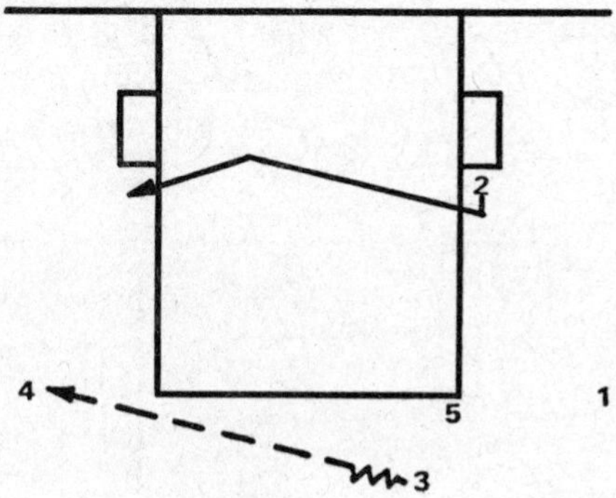

Diagram 6-16

pass in his shooting range. 4 posts up inside if 2 doesn't have his shot and is ready for 2's pass to him. (See Diagram 6-13.)

With the ball in 2's possession (see Diagram 6-14) the double screen is set up as 2 reverses the ball to 3 on top. When this occurs, 2 passes to 3 and 5 slides down the lane to set a double screen with 4. 2 splits the double screen and then 4 and 5 pinch it off as 2 slips through.

If 2 isn't open as he comes off the double screen, 1 can initiate a new option in our 1-5 series. (See Diagram 6-15.) Again, 1 can either dribble out or pass out to 3. Which move he makes is predetermined by our coaching staff according to the abilities of our second guard. Most of the time we allow the pass. As 1 either passes or dribbles on top, 4 steps out from 5's screen. 5 flashes to the high post area, and 2 can either hold or cross opposite. By holding, 2 can be open on a post-up move as the pass is made by 3 to 4. (See Diagram 6-16.)

Remember, with the ball on top 3 can change to another series if he so desires.

HIGH-LOW POST INTERCHANGE

There are times when, due to pressure on your 3 and 4 players, the middle is opened up for your post interchange. (See Diagram 6-17.) What we are trying to do here is open up the middle even more by taking 3's and 4's defensive players higher. We know that the rule of pressure defense is to force and deny your entry pass to your wings, 3 and 4. So take them higher and open up the middle for 2 and 5 to work.

5 screens down on 2's defensive man while 2 head and shoulder fakes to set his man up for screen. 1 must pass the ball to 2 as he *comes off* 5's screen. After receiving 1's pass, 2 shapes up to the basket ready to shoot, pass, or drive. This is a quick-hitting play, with no basic pattern involved.

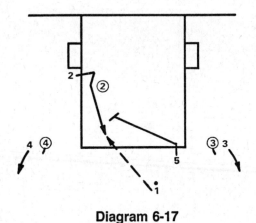

Diagram 6-17

DIRECT INSIDE PASS

Again, when 1 sees defensive pressure on his wings, he should get the ball directly inside to 2 on the blocks. This may seem too simple to work, but it does. If you are able to get the ball into that high percentage area with a pass by 1, do so. (See Diagram 6-18.)

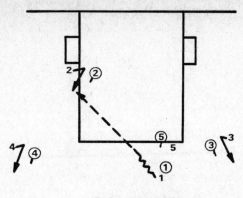

Diagram 6-18

Due to the pressure on 4 by his defensive man, there is a natural pocket created for 2 to step into. 2 should always be alert for this opportunity against a pressure defense. What you must teach 2 here is to get his defensive man on his hip and then seal him there. It is at this juncture that 1 wants to get that ball inside to 2. 1 has to set up his passing angle by dribble driving to a spot near the edge of the lane. Upon receiving the pass, 2 should utilize his power moves to get his shot off.

HIGH POST FEED

Another way of getting the high inside percentage shot is via the high post feed. Again, whenever the defense is pressuring, it helps to open up the inside. Most teams do not have five outstanding defensive players. Also, most big players, 6′4″ to 6′6″ or larger, are only average on defense. The high post feed affords a team the luxury of a safety outlet to the high post. We believe in using our 5 man as a safety valve whenever our offensive people are in trouble. In this case, though, we are using him to enable your team to get the ball inside. (See Diagram 6-19.)

5 wants to be sure to step out to receive the pass from 1. 5 should look inside by pivoting away from his defensive man's pressure. Seeing 1's pass into 5, 2 should use head and shoulder fakes as well as a jab step to set his defensive man up for his move. Seeing his defensive

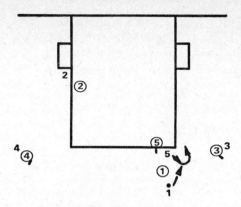

Diagram 6-19

man playing tight and high, 2 should try to get open low. The reverse is true if 2's defensive man is playing low. In the event 2's defensive man is playing loose, 2 should go to him before making his move. Sometimes when 2 is too loose and conscious of 5 looking in he may turn his head. 5 can then use the lob pass to 2 inside.

2's post up moves will be detailed in the drill section at close of this chapter.

REBOUNDING ASSIGNMENTS

As in all our previous play series, all rebounding assignments remain the same in the 2 play series.

We will illustrate several situations where you can follow the application of our rebounding rules.

We will review our rules for rebounding with the ball in 2's hands coming off 1's cross screen (see Diagram 6-1). (See Diagram 6-20.) 2 rebounds ball-side on the blocks, and 5 rebounds help-side on the blocks. 3 rebounds ball-side on the line of 45°. 4 rebounds at the line of 45° help-side. 1's responsibilities remain the same—go to the midpoint area or deep position.

Whether 1 goes deep depends on whether we send all five players to the offensive boards or only four and a half to the boards. Against some teams who are not a threat to run against, we would crash all five players. Of course, by sending all five players you can better contain

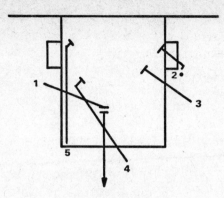

Diagram 6-20

your opponent's fastbreak. It is in areas like this coaches can get gray hairs. The decision as to what to do must be based upon your philosophy, your material, your opponent's material, and the scouting reports on your opponents.

Let's take another situation in the 2 series where 3 has received a pass from 1. Remember that 3 is coming off the shuffle cut and has taken the shot. (See Diagram 6-21.) 3 rebounds his shot at the ball-side position on the blocks. The rule for 3 and 4 is to rebound on the blocks at ball-side only when they have taken the shot from that position.

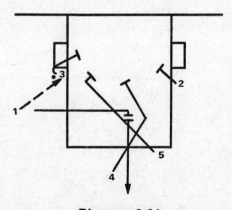

Diagram 6-21

Otherwise, they always rebound on the line of 45°. With this rule established, whoever is at the high post position, generally 5 or 2, would then rebound on the line of 45° ball-side, never help-side. The reason for this becomes apparent when you realize that we always have 2 or 5 on the blocks opposite. With this rule we always have our two strongest rebounders opposite each other.

2 rebounds help-side on the blocks, and 5 goes to the line of 45° ball-side. 4 rebounds help-side on the line of 45°. 1 goes to the mid-point area or deep position.

To reiterate the importance of offensive rules on rebounding: They afford your offensive players the opportunity of knowing beforehand where their responsibilities are, which increases their anticipation. The result is a quicker reaction so that they can, as the saying goes, "be there first with the mostest."

Diagram 6-22 explains how our rebounding rules hold if 1 takes the shot as 3 comes off his shuffle cut.

1 follows his rule and goes to the mid-point area or deep position. 3 rebounds at the line of 45° ball-side, not on the blocks, since 3 did not shoot. 5 rebounds ball-side on the blocks opposite 2. 2 rebounds help-side on the blocks. 4 rebounds help-side on the line of 45°.

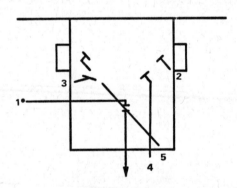

Diagram 6-22

TRANSITION ASSIGNMENTS

In our entire offensive concept transition is another important phase that has certain basic assignments. They have been defined for you in the preceding chapters. We will review them as they pertain to our 2 play series. Remember, they are the same for our entire offensive system.

In this sequence of our 2 play, 5 has jammed the rebounder. He follows his rule and runs a streak pattern to the blocks opposite the ball-side position.

Since 2 is the off rebounder, he crosses through the nearest mid-court passing lane. Remember, we want to cross through the passing lanes since it sets up interceptions. Turnovers in the transition game kill your opponents' just-gained momentum.

4 rebounds ball-side (2 took the shot) at the line of 45° and crosses through 5's outlet passing lane, hesitates, and runs to the next deepest receiver and then to the middle of lane if receiver has not received a pass.

3 crosses 5's passing lane and heads to the deepest receiver opposite the rebounder. 3 then heads to the foul line area, picking up the nearest open man.

1 heads up court to be as deep as their deepest player, who in this case is number 3.

Whenever a player enters an open man area—one with no opposing player—his rule is to cross back through the next passing lane and find the next nearest open receiver while continuing down court.

PRACTICE DRILLS FOR OUR INSIDE POWER 2 PLAY SERIES

Our practice drills are a reflection of our philosophy of teaching by repetition. It is through practice drills that we develop the reactions that make our players respond automatically to each situation. Every drill is practiced with great intensity.

Drill 6-1: Power Moves Inside

Instructions: 3 passes the ball to 2, who is coming across the lane. Later we add a defensive man to 2. Run this drill to both sides. Rotate players as desired.

Teaching Points: 3 must learn to make his pass to 2 at the proper time. The proper time is a split second before 2 is to break open. Also, 2 must receive the pass on balance and ready to make his power moves. Now comes the most important phase—the execution of these inside power moves. Without them your inside game will

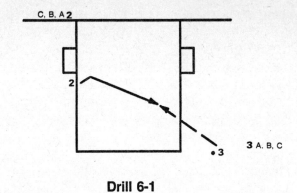

Drill 6-1

be less than successful. I will cover in detail the moves we work on and demand our players to master.

1. *Pump Fake:* After catching the ball, 2 must be sure to keep his defensive man sealed on his hip. We want the ball close to the chin and shoulder so that as he is turning into the defensive man he is protecting the ball. As the pump fakes the ball with head and shoulder fakes, be sure he keeps his knees flexed and does not show more than half of the ball. He can pump one, two, three, or more times. What is important is for him to explode up once he has gotten his opponent off balance. To explode properly he must have his knees in a flexed position. Most young players make a critical error; they tend to straighten their knees as they repeat the pump fake.

2. *Drop step:* As you catch the pass, you must seal the defensive man on your hip. He is generally playing you on the baseline side or on the high-side since he had to fight through a pick. At this point, your offensive man drops his inside foot (the one nearest the three-second lane) on a direct line to the basket (we are assuming the defensive man is playing on the baseline side). The important thing is the angle at which he drops his foot. The tendency here is to step laterally too much. Drill 6-1a shows this move executed correctly and executed incorrectly.

3. *Combination Power Move:* This is simply a combination of pump fakes with the drop step. The player pump fakes one way and drop steps the other.

4. *Slide Bounce Step:* Whenver a player receives a pass and a defensive man is caught on the high-side, this move is avail-

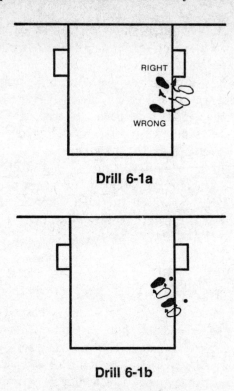

Drill 6-1a

Drill 6-1b

able. Your player should seal the defensive man on his hip and slide both feet using a one-bounce dribble to position for the power layup. This is the only time we allow a dribble, to the baseline side. The reason is simple. There is no defensive help when you're facing a baseline. Help only occurs when you pivot into the middle. This is where those little guards use their quick hands to steal the ball, which is why you do not want the ball put on the floor in this danger area. Drill 6-1b shows how this move should be completed.

5. *Crossover, Turn-Around Jumper, Power Layout, Reverse Layup* (with either hand), *Turn Shot, Hook Shot*. These are some of the moves available to your players. They are already well known to coaches today. Therefore I will not go into detail for these particular moves. Many are used in combination with each other or separately. Of major concern is to master the fundamentals of each move.

Time Sequence: Early in the season we devote ten minutes to this drill. Later in the season we cut the time to five minutes and then to two to three minutes.

Practice Pressure: In early season work, with no defensive pressure being applied and in the early teaching stage, no pressure is used. Later, as fundamentals have been mastered, we apply pressure. With a defensive man, 2 must execute four out of five moves correctly and score four out of five times. If the defense is successful two times or more, the offense loses; otherwise, the defense loses. In this type of teaching drill, the winner accumulates points—whatever you wish to award—toward being excused from running gut drills at the conclusion of practice. The loser runs.

Drill 6-2: Cross Screen

Instructions: 1 passes to 3, jab steps, and rubs off 5's screen, crossing the lane to screen for 2. 3 shapes up to basket ready to pass, shoot, or drive. 2 head and shoulder feints his man and then rubs off 1's screen. We start with 1, 3, and 2 and add 5 later. Defense is added to 2 and then to 1, 3, and 5. This is done when you feel your players are ready for it. Rotate players as desired. Change to 4's side of floor on alternate days.

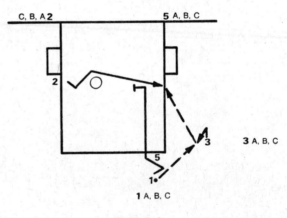

Drill 6-2

Teaching Points: 1 must make his pass to 3's outside target hand. He must set a correct screen and release properly. 2 must use proper fakes and time his cut to 1's screen-cut. 2 must rub his man off tight. 2 must be on balance and use proper inside power moves. 3 must pass to 2 at the proper moment and with the correct pass, most often the bounce pass.

Time Sequence: Early in the season we work for eight minutes. In midseason, we work four minutes. Late in the season, we work two minutes.

Practice Pressure: In early season work the pressure is applied through time. We allow five to three seconds, cutting time down as we go. It is important to properly execute the fundamentals and still be *quick*! If the drill is done improperly or too slowly three out of four times, they run. If they do it right, they are finished with the drill. Later in the season the pressure is applied competitively. The losers run; vary the type of running.

Drill 6-3: Shuffle Cut

Instructions: Start with no defensive players and then add defensive players to 3, 5, 1, and 4, in that order. 1 passes to and rubs off 5. 1 pauses to set an imaginary screen and then goes on. 5 recrosses to butt screen for 3's shuffle cut. Rotate players as desired, from

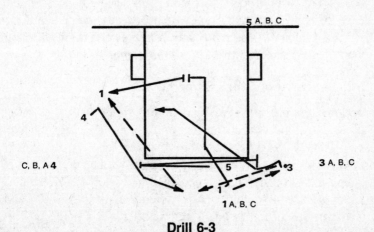

Drill 6-3

offense to defense. On alternate days of practice, run the drill to the opposite side of court.

Teaching Points: Remind 1 to jab step to set his defensive man up. 1 must set a proper screen. Meanwhile, 3 must use head and shoulder fakes before rubbing his man off 5's butt screen. Make sure 3 goes by 5's hip tight. 5 must set two correct butt screens, one for 4, who is rotating up, and then one for 3. 4 wants to brush tight to 5's outside hip as he rotates to the head of circle. After running the shuffle cut, 3 looks to receive the pass from 1. He should be on balance and ready to make his offensive move. 1 must be sure to make the proper pass to 3 so that 3 will not have to catch the ball off balance or too late. This is *critical timing*.

Time Sequence: We work ten minutes early in the season. In midseason we cut the time to six minutes. In late season we cut the time to three minutes.

Practice Pressure: The players being guarded must execute the drill properly two out of three, three out of four, or four out of five times. The losers run. Players not being guarded are allowed no mistakes or they run. When the drill reaches a four-on-four situation, the defense is allowed to fastbreak on all opportunities, less made shots. In this situation, we play a six-, eight-, or ten-point game. The rules are as follows: The defense is awarded a point for each turnover, rebound, and fastbreak with a three-on-two situation or better, plus two points for scoring on a transition break. The offense scores two points for a score plus one point for each offensive rebound. The offense keeps the ball after each successful score. Losers run, and winners get a drink. Sometimes we will play a best-two-out-of-three game.

Drill 6-4: Reverse Cross Screen by 3

Instructions: We pre-set 1 and 4 where they would normally end up. 3 passes to 4 and runs a shuffle cut. When 3 does not receive the pass from 1, he reverses to cross screen for 2 on the blocks. 1 then passes to 2 as he breaks open. Start with a defensive man on 2 and then add defensive men to 2 and later 1. Rotate players from offense to defense. Add defensive men to 3, 2, and 5. Switch sides of the floor on alternate days.

Teaching Points: Emphasize 3's shuffle cut and the proper screening

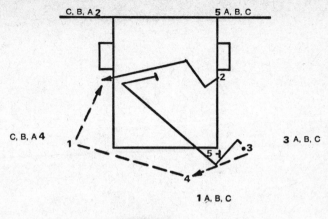

Drill 6-4

for 2. 2 must set his man up and time his cut to rub off 3's screen as close as possible. 1 must be told repeatedly to make his pass a split second before 2 breaks open and to put the ball in there so 2 can receive the pass on balance and ready to use his power moves. Emphasize 2's use of the bounce pass.

Time Sequence: Early in the season we work for eight minutes. In midseason we cut the time to five minutes. Late in the season time is reduced to two minutes.

Practice Pressure: The offense must succeed two out of three, three out of four, or four out of five times. The defense stays on defense until they succeed in stopping the offense from this accomplishment.

Drill 6-5: Skip Pass

Instructions: The ball is in 3's hands. 3 runs his cut. 5 butt screens for 4 and returns for a second butt screen. 1 swings up to receive a pass from 4. The defense denies 3's possible pass receivers as best they can. 3 must skip pass to whoever is open. Defense is played tough on 4, 1, and 5. Rotate offense to defense as desired. Change sides of floor on alternate days.

Teaching Points: It is important to teach 3 to read and react to our opponents defensive pressure. I am not forgetting 4's, 1's, or 5's ability to read and react. This area must be stressed as well. We

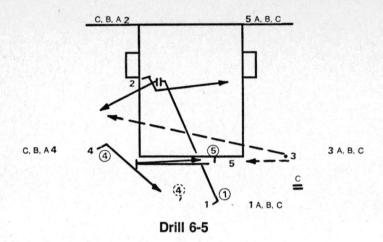

Drill 6-5

will sometimes have a coach stand so as to indicate to the defensive players who we want to get open. This is done to see if 3 is taking in the entire picture. If he is seeing the whole picture, he will recognize the situation immediately and make the correct choice. Who receives the pass determines how the 2 play will be run.

Time Sequence: We work eight minutes early in the season. We reduce the time to four minutes in the middle of the season, and later we reduce the time to two minutes.

Practice Pressure: We rotate the 3 men, giving each player one attempt at a time. They may go through the drill three to six times. The pressure on them is produced if any one of them selects the wrong pass. They (the 3 men) run. The same is true for the 4 men when the drill is run to 4's side. What this helps to create is teamwork by each teammate who is fighting for the same position. If defense doesn't succeed in their efforts at least twice, they run. If 4, 1, 5, or 2 do not execute the fundamentals properly (coaches decision) they run.

7

The Inside Power

Rotation Theory

Against Zone Defenses

ZONE DEFENSE—ITS THEORY
AND APPLICATION

Before we can attack something it is often prudent to try and understand just what it is you are attacking. Otherwise, it could be like Lord Tennyson's *Charge of the Light Brigade* ". . . . Into the valley of death rode the 500. . . ." As brave as it might be, this style of attack would surely lead to disaster.

Where in previous years your team might have faced man-to-man defense most of the time and zone defense only a few times, it is now faced with a multitude of complex defenses. Coaches have taken the standard zones and done some amazing things with them.

Yes, times have changed. No longer do you face a zone that plays you straight up. Zones will, for our purposes, fall into three basic categories or styles: (1) the Standard Perimeter Zones, (2) the Pressure Zones, and (3) the Flex-Matchup Zones. Coaches must come up with offenses against them. Because of the significant differences in these types of zone defense, offensive strategy must not be predictable. The problem lies in developing a simple yet diversified offensive system able to handle all of these zones.

What we have tried to do is establish a few basic concepts for an offensive system. A system flexible enough to be able, with various adjustments, to handle the various zones—one that remains simple, yet gives us flexibility in our offensive patterns and a minimum of passing—one that works for the good, close-in, high-percentage shot.

CONCEPTS OF ZONE STYLES

What follows is a brief description of the zone defenses you will be faced with defeating. You must have some knowledge of what you are trying to attack before you charge ahead. When you understand the premise a particular defense such as a zone defense is working under, you can attain much greater success against it.

The Standard Perimeter Zones

All traditional zone defenses, such as the 2-3, 1-3-1, 3-2, 1-2-2, and the 2-1-2, try to protect the inside and give you the perimeter shots—hence the name, perimeter zones. The three-second area is this zone defense's primary concern. The defensive players on the perimeter not guarding the ball must sag into the three-second area. Their purpose is to deny the pass from your outside players to your inside players. Sometimes, if you have an outstanding perimeter shooter, they will pressure the ball when he has it. Sometimes they just pressure whoever has the ball on the perimeter.

The Pressure Zones

These zones have the same basic alignments as the perimeter zones. The major difference is the pressure the defenders apply in attempting to push the offense out while pressuring the passing lanes. With pressure on the ball, the nearest receiver will be denied the pass. This defense is more aggressive and risky. While the perimeter protects the inside, the pressure zone attacks the perimeter, leaving some openings inside. What they hope to gain is confusion on your part by disrupting your offensive patterns. If this occurs, turnovers quickly follow. Soon there is no penetration, just frustration.

The Flex-Match Up Zones

The flex-match up zones are the latest innovation. Even though they have been with us for a while, their sophistication has made flex-match up zones tough to deal with. What the flex-match up zone expects to do is play you consistently in a one-on-one situation with a zone concept. This one-on-one game is a man-to-man game, where one man guards a man in his area, but not a specific man. He will not guard a player unless he is in his defensive area. He will not follow him all over the court. Thus, the flex-match up zone can maintain the formation of your offense. This match up is tough on overloads and set patterns. Patterns that use movement by cuts only can be matched up. Flex-match up zones are generally extended from the perimeter zones.

Zone identification is important to your players. I especially believe in teaching our guards how to read the type of zone defense we are facing. Any team that knows what it is facing gains confidence, which is an advantage in what you are attempting to accomplish.

DEVELOPING A ZONE OFFENSIVE SYSTEM

With the understanding we have of zone defensive theory, we can develop a precise method of attack. We desired a system that has movement, both ball and man, screening, and penetration leading to the high percentage shot.

As in our man-to-man offense, it is our belief that our players must be able to *read and react to the defense*. In other words, instead of allowing the defense to dictate to us, we intend to dictate to it.

To our way of thinking a zone offense must be as close to your man-to-man offense as possible. There are similarities in today's two principle defenses. Man-to-man defense has zone principles; for example, its help-side players sag to cut off any penetration and shut off the passing lanes and players jump in and switch on cutters. Zone defenses, by denial of passing lanes and going one-on-one with a cutter or dribbler, are attempting to use much the same techniques.

Therefore, your passing fundamentals are of as much importance in attacking zones as in attacking man-to-man. Zones require less one-on-one ability and are easier to get open against, but they do demand top-flight passing to get open against. Though minimal passing is emphasized, our pass selection is probably more vital to success overall. Thus, passing becomes a priority item in developing your zone attack. Today's coaches spend far too little time on the passing game. There is only one way to accomplish good passing, and that is by drilling.

A man-to-man offense requires precise movement, and a zone

offense requires movement of a similar nature to create openings in the zone defense without movement. A zone defense, or for that matter any defense, can stay with your first or even second move. It is the third or fourth move that disorients the defense.

So now we introduce another term, one we have mentioned before, called patience. How many mistakes will a defense make in four or five seconds? What happens when you move man and ball to the reverse side and back again or inside and back outside? The defense must crack and weaken, leading to errors. What is important to your offense is to be patient until this defensive lapse occurs. Then your players must capitalize on the defensive mistakes.

Now you must create space to work. The defense must be forced to cover as much floor space as possible. You do this by playing the zone defense as if it were an accordian: Compress it and then expand it. In doing this you create open passing lanes. When the defense spreads, you must step into the gaps of the zone. When the defense is compressed, you must step outside the gaps but be in your shooting range.

To spread the zone properly, you must cross court the ball against the zone to take advantage of openings on the backside. This forces the zone to cover more floor space than it is capable of, as quickly as possible. Again, use the principle of the accordian—expand and compress. The cracks in the defense will present themselves. We refer to this offensive move as skip passing. What this means is that you miss a man as you reverse the ball. You might even skip two players. Our sole objective is to get the ball to the open man as quickly as possible.

Inside Game

In building our offense against the zone, the Inside Power Game becomes the critical factor. You must maintain offensive pressure in the low and high post areas. This is very easy to say but extremely difficult to execute. We must penetrate with the ball into the defensive interior, or heart, of the zone.

How is this accomplished? There are several methods of penetration. The one used most often is the direct pass into the heart of the defense. Another method is one many coaches have used over the years—*the drive*. This is a mandatory technique for us. Our outside players must be aware of this opportunity to penetrate the gaps of the zone with the dribble drive.

Another method is to use the threat of the dribble drive but pull up

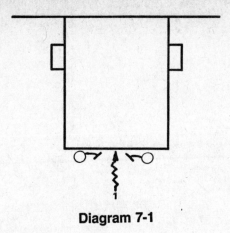

Diagram 7-1

after the defense commits two defensive players to stopping the driver's penetration. We call this dribble penetration. Penetration here is vital since the defense is playing five-on-four, and at an obvious advantage. Our guard, seeing no defender on the ball, must split the defenders. (See Diagram 7-1.) Now when the defense commits two defenders to stopping the ball's penetration, the offense has a four-on-three advantage in personnel against the remaining interior defensive players.

The *passing angle dribble* is another method of attaining a better penetration pass. This technique has the offensive 1, 3, or 4 man taking one or two dribbles to create a better passing angle into the post areas. (See Diagram 7-2.)

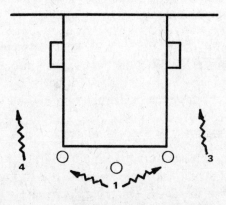

Diagram 7-2

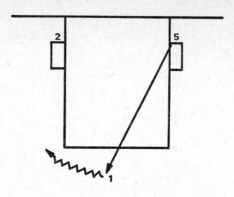

Diagram 7-3

Our dribble rotation lends variety to our offensive series. By driving hard at the wing position, 1 creates problems for the flex-match up and pressure zones. Either 5 or 2, whoever is on the opposite side, flashes on top to fill 1's spot. (See Diagram 7-3.)

The *high post pass* creates a different set of problems for the defense. When the high post receives a pass, he must immediately look inside to the low post or wing area. This move hits the defense where they have no help-side help. This pass can be a valuable adjunct to your overall offensive concepts against zones.

Screening

I believe in screening against zones whenever possible within your ball and man movement. The flexibility you must develop in your players' screening techniques is where they are to screen. Screening against a zone requires your players to seek out the most logical player who would be assigned to cover the area you are screening to open up. As in man-to-man defense, the screener must open to the ball after screening. He is often left open momentarily when the zone shifts to meet this new problem. Screening adds to the problems of the flex-match ups and perimeter zones when they try to adjust to it.

Point Guard Responsibilities—1 Man

The number one responsibility for our point guard (1 man) is to keep the offense moving. Anytime your offense stagnates you are in trouble. By keeping the offense moving, our point guard forces the defense to be in constant motion. Constant motion by the defense will eventually result in a mistake by a defensive player. The offense must be ready to take advantage of this mistake.

Most important is the mental posture of your point guard. By this I mean the ability to continue to look for other open players so he can get them the ball. At the same time, 1 must be able to realize when he has the shot. 1 must look for his teammate's opening, yet be quick enough to recognize his own.

Since penetration is a major goal in our offense, it becomes critical for our 1 man to be alert to penetrating the defense. He must also keep the other perimeter players aware of the possibilities of penetration by pass, drive, or dribble pinch. Our 1 man must also be sure to keep our post men moving to enable the penetrating pass to be made.

In other words, the point guard must exert himself to keep the offense moving. His ability to read the defensive posture and make the offensive adjustments necessary will go a long way to determine your team's success each season. When he does not have the ball, your 1 man should be observing what the defense is doing. This enables him to react more quickly. Remember, our 1 man is always the deepest defender. His responsibility is to stop your opponent's fastbreak. You must teach your point guard well. He is an extension of you on the floor.

Perimeter or Wing Responsibilities—3 and 4 Men

The wings (our 3 and 4 men) must always be wide enough to be open and a stride above the zone's perimeter wing defensive players. (See Diagram 7-4.) This facilitates your entry pass from the point guard. It is important for your wings to understand the point guard's (1 man) responsibilities since this helps the 3 and 4 men in their penetration role.

Our 4 and 3 men must be alert to see when the cut is available to them. When there is a gap in the defense, they should look to penetrate into it or these motion-producing moves would be wasted.

As with our 1 man, 3 and 4 must remember to be observant of the post movement against the interior defense. When a post man (5 or 2 player) moves into a vacant spot, we want the 3 and 4 wings to see this and be able to penetrate inside with a direct pass.

The rules we have for rebounding in our man-to-man offense remain basically the same against zones. The 3 and 4 wings are responsible for rebounding inside, and our 5 and 2 are post men. 1 man is

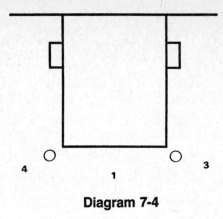

Diagram 7-4

mid-point rebounder or deep safety, as determined before or during the game.

Inside Post Responsibilities

What is our objective? To get the ball inside the heart of the zone. The post area is the danger zone for the defense. If a breakdown occurs in this area, the zone is in for a hard time. Hence, we are back to our first objective: The offensive post men (5 and 2) must be able to get open.

The offense must be able to penetrate, and one of the principle methods is the direct pass. To accomplish this there are several moves our 5 and 2 men must execute if they are to get open very often. 5 and 2 must rotate on each pass into the wing position or reversal of the ball. To do this, 5 and 2 should rotate in a circular motion toward the flow of the ball. On all ball reversals, including skip passes, 5 and 2 should "X" their moves. (See Diagram 7-5.) It is imperative that 5 and 2 understand the importance of this movement. They must move and not stand on the blocks all night.

We want our 5 and 2 men to act as a two-man unit within the framework of the team unit. Communication with each other during the course of the game is extremely important. By functioning in this manner, 5 and 2 can avoid standing in the same position where one defensive player can cover two offensive players. They must always try to stay opposite each other. What this accomplishes is very important to any offensive team—rebounding. Since the zone defense has a tougher job blocking out, 5 and 2 have a better opportunity in their

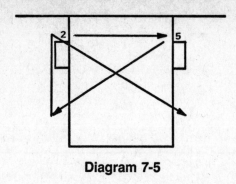

Diagram 7-5

rebounding assignments. Even with this advantage, your players must *want* the ball. No matter what else is said and done, rebounding is the name of the game. At this juncture we are now ready to apply the principles we have discussed previously in this chapter.

BASIC OFFENSIVE SET

The principles discussed so far in this chapter are just the parts that must be put together to form the sum total. Our basic alignment is out of a 1-2-2 set, moving into a 1-3-1 and back to a 1-2-2 overload. (See Diagram 7-6.) 1 is at the point position. Our 3 and 4 players are at the perimeter or wing positions. Their alignment is the foul line ex-

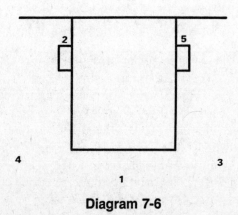

Diagram 7-6

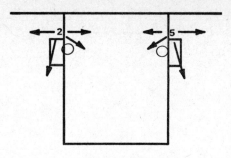

Diagram 7-7

tended and one step above the defensive perimeter players. In the interior of the zone, 5 and 2 must align themselves directly behind the zone's interior defensive players. In doing this, they have placed an added burden on the inside defensive people. Since they cannot see 5 and 2, the defensive players have a more difficult time trying to defeat 5's and 2's moves into the gaps. (See Diagram 7-7.)

As the ball is moved around the perimeter, the interior defense must shift to meet the new angle of ball pressure. At the same time they must be aware of where 5 and 2 are. Thus, 5 and 2 are afforded that vital moment of indecision by the defense as to what open area they will break into.

It should be obvious by now that our offensive power is concentrated on the high percentage area in our zone offense, as it is in our man-to-man offense. Our entire system is based on this approach. But part of any offensive success revolves around the art of offensive rebounding.

REBOUNDING ASSIGNMENTS

Our zone offensive rebounding assignments do not vary from the man-to-man ones. The rules are as follows: 5 and 2 rebound on the blocks opposite each other, 3 and 4 rebound on the line of 45°, and 1 has the mid-point area or deep safety. We do adjust 1's rebounding assignment more than any of the others, because 1 has a straight-in vertical shot down the gut of the defense. Few zones are able to adequately block out this rebounding move.

In Diagram 7-8 our rebounding rules are reviewed. The ball has been reversed on top to 4 from 1. The shot is taken by 4. 5 rebounds on

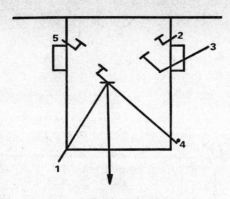

Diagram 7-8

the blocks opposite help-side, and 2 rebounds ball-side on the blocks. 4 rebounds on the line of 45° help-side, and 3 rebounds at the line of 45° ball-side. 1 rebounds down the gut or goes to the mid-point or deep safety.

Again, it is imperative for each offensive player to anticipate his teammate's shot. It is with this anticipation and a desire to rebound with intensified abandon that a team achieves outstanding rebounding accomplishments.

Let us look at another sequence where 3 takes a shot on the baseline as the ball was reversed after the initial movement. (See Diagram 7-9.) 2 has rotated to the blocks opposite while 5 flashed to the open area. Seeing that 1 is taking the shot, 5 heads for the rebound area on the blocks ball-side. 4, who rotated up on the backside of the

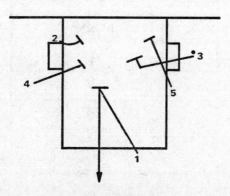

Diagram 7-9

zone, rebounds help-side on the line of 45°. 3 rebounds ball-side on the line of 45°, and 1 rebounds vertically down the seam or mid-point or deep safety position.

TRANSITION ASSIGNMENTS

Once the shot is airborne, you are in a gray area between offense and defense, and it is here that many games have been won or lost. Having gone to the offensive boards with a relaxed abandon to attain that second and third shot and failed, you are now in a transition to your defensive perimeter. The perimeter could be full court, third court, half court, or less, but you must be organized getting there.

Diagram 7-10 will illustrate our rules of transition as applied to our zone offense. As discussed in previous chapters, our transition rules remain constant. The numbered players that are shown as circles in Diagram 7-10 are our offensive players being depicted as defensive since we are now considering ourselves as being on defense. The ball has been rebounded by our opponents. 2, who is the nearest to the rebounder, follows his rule and jams the rebounder. After delaying the outlet pass, 2 runs a streak pattern to the blocks opposite the ball-side. This is the rule for whoever jams the rebounder. 5 is the help-side rebounder. He crosses through the nearest mid-court passing lane,

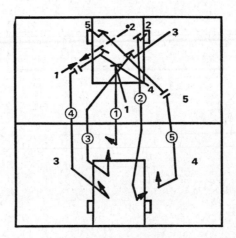

Diagram 7-10

pauses, and then goes onto the next deepest receiver. 1 is on top. He follows his rule by being as deep as the deepest player, who is number 3. 4 is the help-side rebounder at the line of 45°. He crosses 2's outlet passing lane, hesitates, and runs to the next deepest receiver and then to the middle of the lane. 3 crosses 2's passing lane heading to the deepest receiver opposite the rebounder. 3 then heads for the foul line area, picking up the nearest open man.

Whenever a player enters an open man area—one with no opposing player—his rule is to cross back through the next passing lane and find the next nearest open receiver while continuing down court.

PRACTICE DRILLS FOR OUR ZONE INSIDE POWER ROTATION OFFENSE

Our practice drills for developing our zone offense are no different in intensity than those used in teaching man-to-man principles. We are trying to develop the reactions that enable our players to respond automatically to each situation that arises. The ability to read and react is developed much more quickly by repetition and intense practice.

Drill 7-1: 3 Man Penetration

Instructions: 1, 3, and 4 try to penetrate the defense. They want to force two defensive players to cover one in trying to stop the penetration. 1 penetrates, followed by 3 and then 4. The other

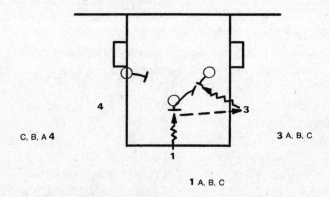

Drill 7-1

two players step to the pocket. Rotate new players in as desired. The offense rotates to defense.

Teaching Points: 1 must make the middle man of zone commit to him by driving at him and then into the gap. If 1 can go all the way, he should. 1 must have his head up and always be looking to pass to the open man when he has forced the defense to commit 2 men to stop him. Players 3 and 4 must move to open areas created by this pinch move of defense. The penetrator, 1, 3, or 4, should keep his feet on the floor when he is passing. Only if he is taking it to the iron should he leave his feet. The penetrator must put his pass into the receiver's hands so he can shoot quickly or drive. The pass receiver must always be on balance and ready to shoot. He must be squared up when he receives the pass. We like to use the bounce pass most of the time.

Time Sequence: We work ten minutes early in the season. In mid-season we cut the time to five minutes. Late in the season we cut the time to three to five minutes.

Practice Pressure: Each group is allowed 60 seconds to work. No mistakes are allowed. This means that all passes must be where the receiver can catch them on balance and ready to shoot. All receivers must be on balance and squared up. The total number of mistakes made are the number of sprints run. Pluses cancel out minuses.

Drill 7-2: 3 Man Rotate

Instructions: The point guard initiates movement by attacking the defense or passing to 3 or 4. This drill is similar to the penetration drill except that we now add the diagonal cut by our wings. Each wing man (3 or 4) must cut after he handles the ball. Rotate the offense to defense when you bring in three new players on offense.

Teaching Points: There are several key teaching points. First, the passer must read the defense and make the proper response to it. Second, the wings must cut properly. They (3 and 4) must look for the defensive opening and go for it. Also, they must hesitate on their cut when they are open to allow the passer time to get them the ball. Again, they must be on balance and ready to shoot upon receiving the pass. Third, 3 and 4 must widen out on their cut as they come up the backside of zone.

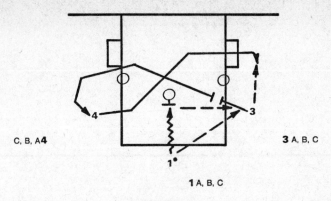

C, B, A**4**   **3** A, B, C

1 A, B, C

Drill 7-2

Time Sequence: We work ten minutes early in the season. We work seven minutes in midseason. Later the time is cut to five or three minutes.

Practice Pressure: The offense must be successful on five, seven, or nine straight passes. The defense wins if the offense doesn't succeed. Passes must be correct, and diagonal cuts must be properly made. Total mistakes go against the offense. Whatever point total you set determines winners or losers.

Drill 7-3: Post Rotate

Instructions: 1, 3, and 4 are not allowed to shoot in this drill. Their purpose is to get the ball inside to 5 or 2. 1, 3, or 4 may fake the penetration move, but primarily they are to work on their direct pass inside. 3 and 4 may skip pass occasionally to work on this phase. 5 and 2 are to flash to the pocket in their inside rotation moves. On ball reversal, they should "X" their moves. Rotate offensive 1, 3, and 4 men to the defense and replace them with new 2 and 5 men.

Teaching Points: What is important to emphasize here is that 2 and 5 must go to the open area and, upon catching a pass, turn and face the basket to make their offensive move. Also, 5 and 2 should look to kick the ball to the backside of the defense when the interior defense pinches in on them. It is important to emphasize 5's and 2's timing of their cuts and constant movement. Emphasize attacking the offensive boards when either one of them shoots.

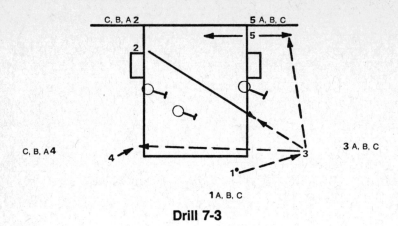

Drill 7-3

Time Sequence: We work ten minutes early in the season. We work seven minutes in midseason. Later in the season we work five or three minutes.

Practice Pressure: One of the inside post players, either 2 or 5, must get open on every third pass. The defense wins if they cause a turnover or force an extra pass by the offense. 2 and 5 stay on offense as long as they are successful. If 2 and 5 succeed three straight times, they are allowed to bank one bonus point. At end of practice they can exercise their banked bonus points and be excused from running sprints, or they may accumulate them to be used later. If 2 and 5 fail, they run and two more players take their places.

8

Inside Power Rotation

Against Zone Defenses

Theory must now be transferred into practical application. In this chapter we discuss the inside power rotation offense and how it functions. What follows is a precise description of how we deploy and attack with ball and man movement against perimeter, pressure, and flex-match up zones.

BASIC INSIDE POWER ROTATION OFFENSE

All initial movement is keyed by 1's moves, by pass, dribble rotation, dribble penetration (pinch), or a direct pass to high post.

Let's examine our basic movement against the perimeter zones. 1 starts the offense with the entry pass to 4, who is at the left wing against a 2-1-2 zone. (See Diagram 8-1.) As the pass is made to 4 by the point guard 1, 3 cuts to baseline left. 5 holds until the interior defense is in the midst of its adjustment to the ball and man movement. 4 has the option of passing to 3 in the corner, making a direct bounce pass to 5, who is flashing to the gap of the defense, or making a dribble penetration (pinch).

On the pass to 3 in the corner, 4 cuts on a diagonal to the blocks and to the backside of the zone. (See Diagram 8-2.) 1 rotates far enough over to be open for 3's reversal pass. 5, who flashed into the gap when 4 had the ball, rolls down the lane behind 4's diagonal cut. 2 crosses to the blocks opposite as 4 passes to 3 in the corner. Prior to 4's pass to 3, 2 had the option of flashing to any open area. (See Diagram 8-3.) If 4 or 3 had taken a perimeter shot, 2 would be the backside

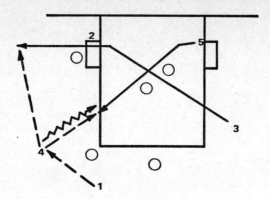

Diagram 8-1

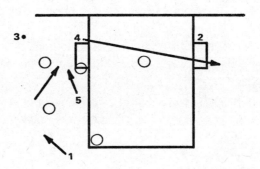

Diagram 8-2

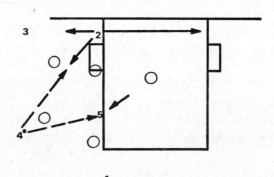

Diagram 8-3

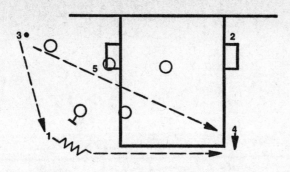

Diagram 8-4

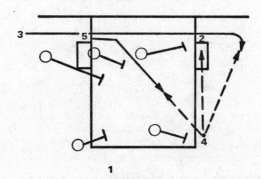

Diagram 8-5

rebounder. Though a perimeter shot is rarely taken on the first or second pass, you must by cuts and ball movement force the defense to commit to a different offensive set.

If 3 was unable to penetrate the interior of the zone with a direct pass, he should quickly reverse the ball to 1 or skip pass to 4 on the backside of the zone. (See Diagram 8-4.) After receiving 3's pass, 1 should reverse the ball as quickly as possible, with one or two dribbles, and pass to 4, who is rotating up the side of the lane on the zone's backside. 4 should catch the pass on balance, shaped up to the basket, and ready to shoot. He should look inside to 2 on the blocks or 3 running the baseline. (See Diagram 8-5.) 5 holds momentarily to time his flash cut. He times his move to the interior defensive players' adjustment to the ball movement and 4's, 2's and 3's cuts.

It is important here to remind your team how important ball rever-

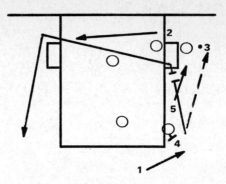

Diagram 8-6

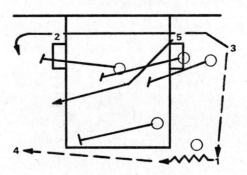

Diagram 8-7

sal is. Remember the accordian effect—expand and compress. As we moved from the original overload position to one of ball reversal to the backside of the zone to the interior, our expanding and compressing effect was accomplished. But if our offense is still not able to penetrate the defense, the motion of ball and man must be repeated. It is this rapid reversal that causes defenders to fail in their shifting assignments.

In Diagram 8-6, the movement of 4, 3, 2, and 5 is repeated to the opposite side of the floor. It is important here for the offense to try to expand the defense as they reshift their assignments in a new direction.

On their rotation, 3 and 4 must widen up, otherwise the defense will not be forced to expand after having been compressed. (See Diagram 8-6.)

In Diagram 8-7, 1 has received the pass from 3 to initiate ball and man reversal. Each player will continue the rotation pattern back to the opposite side of the floor. When your cutters 3 and 4 come out wider on cuts, the help-side defenders must widen the distance between them. This sudden expansion helps to create the defensive errors. As 4 receives 1's pass, he should be on balance, shaped up, and ready to shoot. 4 looks inside for 2 or 5 and toward the corner for 3, who is crossing along the baseline. 5 times his flash move to the shifting of the interior defense.

This basic inside power rotation series is run against all the various zone defensive sets. They are the 1-2-2, 3-2, 1-3-1, and 2-3, plus the perimeter, pressure, and flex-match up zones. This chapter will explain these adjustments of penetration and screening against the various style zones.

Anytime a defensive error occurs in the sequence of the offensive flow as shown in Diagrams 8-1 through 8-7, 1, 3, or 4 must seize on the opportunity immediately. A dribble penetration by 1 at the point position can often occur on ball reversal. (See Diagram 8-8.) 1, 3, and 4 must be alert for the dribble penetration move. I will use the positions shown in Diagram 8-7 for illustrative purposes in Diagram 8-8.

Seeing the help-side defensive man rush out too quickly on his shift, 1 uses a dribble drive or penetration move to the middle of the interior. Seeing 1's penetration move, 4 drops down, but not in, toward the defense, anticipating a drop off pass. We want 4 shaped up and ready to shoot in case he receives 1's pass. 3 starts his baseline cut but, seeing 1's penetration move, reverses his cut to be in a position for

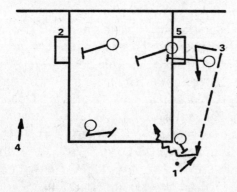

Diagram 8-8

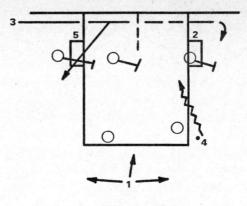

Diagram 8-9

1's drop off pass. Again, 3 must be shaped up to the basket and ready to shoot. 2 and 5 on the blocks try to improve their inside position and be ready for 1's pass or to rebound 1's, 3's, or 4's shot.

Diagram 8-9 shows a dribble drive or penetration move executed by 3 or 4 at the wing position. Using a situation that would occur on a reversal of ball and man movement, as illustrated in Diagram 8-4, 4, seeing he can penetrate the gap into the interior zone defense, does so. If he can take in for a lay up, he will. If the interior defense adjusts, 4 would look to drop off to 5 and 2 on the blocks. Since 5's move is normally to flash, there would seem to be a problem for 4 on his penetration. But remember 5's and 2's rule: Pause before flashing while the zone adjusts to read and react. Thus, what looks like a problem is not really a problem. Having started his baseline cut, 3 reads 4's penetration move and has one of two choices. He can continue his cut to complete the reversal option. This is a must if 3 has reached the mid-point of the three-second lane, which is shown by a dotted line. If 3 hasn't reached the mid-point, he must reverse and pop out to the wing area ready to receive 4's drop off pass. 5 and 2 move for positions on the blocks ready for 4's pass or to rebound. 1 slides to the open spot on the perimeter to be a receiver for 4's pass.

Our basic power rotation series doesn't vary much when it is run against the odd front zones, such as the 1-2-2 or 1-3-1. We will discuss the continuity series as run against the 1-2-2 next.

Diagram 8-10 illustrates the initial movement. 1 must always be alert to the dribble penetration move. Often, 1 can initiate the offense by the dribble penetration move or the threat of it. When 1 accomplishes this move, 4 and 3 often have the gap opened for them to

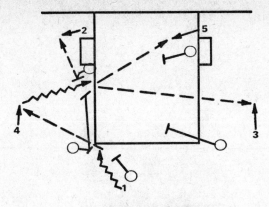

Diagram 8-10

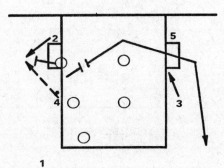

Diagram 8-11

penetrate. When 1 starts the penetration move, 4 and 3 must slide down the sideline to the open area created by 1's penetration but do not close toward defense. To do this would only help the recovery of the defensive man making his shift after he was forced out of his position by 1's penetration. 4 now has the option to shoot a pass to 2, who is stepping out, 5, who is on the blocks, or 3, who is in the crease on the backside.

Since you do not generally obtain the high percentage shot on the first move against a good shifting zone, 4 looks to pass to baseline area. (See Diagram 8-11.) Anytime a wing 4 or 3 makes a dribble penetration move on receiving the entry pass, the offside wings' rule is not to cut through on a baseline move as in the basic pattern of play. The low post on the ball-side steps out on baseline. After passing to 2 on the baseline (see Diagram 8-11), 4 makes his diagonal cut, looking for a return pass from 2.

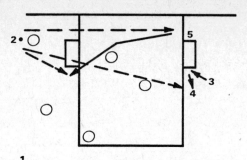

Diagram 8-12

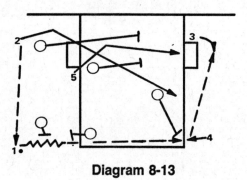

Diagram 8-13

Diagram 8-12 shows the ball baseline in 2's possession. 2 is shaped up and ready to shoot a short baseline. 5 flashes to the opening in the middle of the zone. 3 cuts to the blocks opposite as 4 heads up the lane on the backside. 1 positions himself to be open for 2's pass. 2 looks for 5's flash, 3 on the blocks opposite, or a skip pass to 4 on the backside.

If none of these avenues are open, 2 reverses the ball to 1. (See Diagram 8-13.) 1 looks for a dribble penetration move or a pass to 4, who is coming up to the free throw line extended. 4 immediately looks inside to 2 "Xing" high on a flash cut, 5 crossing low, or 3 running the baseline step out. At this juncture, we are back in the basic pattern of play.

Diagram 8-14 illustrates the basic power rotation moves as depicted earlier, in Diagrams 8-1 through 8-7. 4 chooses to pass to 3 baseline. We encourage this pass often since we feel a zone is hurt when the ball is allowed to get to the baseline area. 4 makes his diagonal cut, making sure he widens out as he comes up the backside

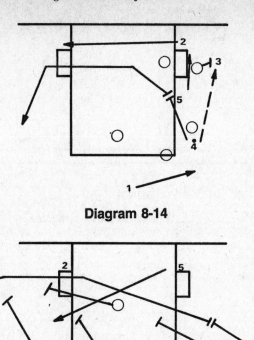

Diagram 8-14

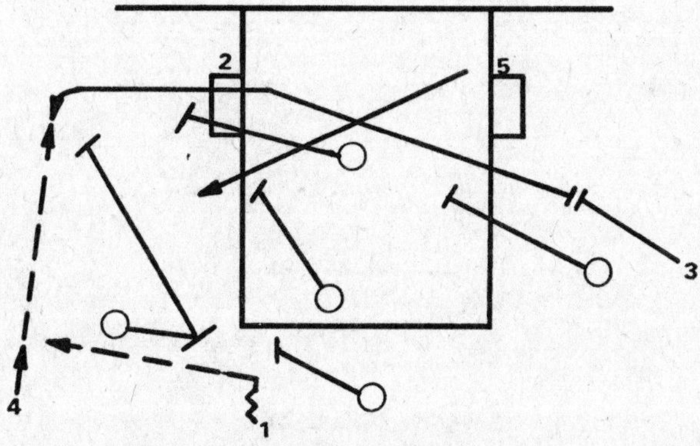

Diagram 8-15

of the zone. 5 cuts off 4's diagonal cut to the opening on the blocks. 2 heads for the blocks opposite, and 1 slides over to be a receiver for 3's pass.

The 1-3-1 perimeter zone creates a slightly different set of problems for our basic rotation. However, we start out with the ball and man movement described previously. Diagram 8-15 illustrates the initial movement. 1 can dribble penetrate, forcing the defense to commit its two players to him, or he can pass directly to 4 or 3. Both 4 and 3 must start a stride above the defensive wings. 1 passes to 4, who looks inside to 2 or 5 flashing. 3 has made his usual cut to the baseline, and 4 passes to 3 in the corner. When you're playing against a 1-3-1 zone, the corners are obviously the open areas to attack but also the areas vulnerable to trapping.

Diagram 8-16 continues the basic pattern of play. After his pass to

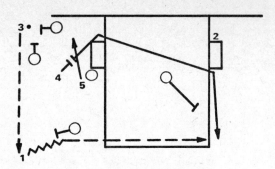

Diagram 8-16

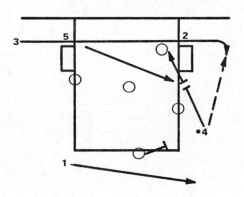

Diagram 8-17

3 on the baseline, 4 cuts diagonally to the blocks looking for a return pass. 5 follows 4's cut to the blocks. 2 clears to the blocks opposite, and 1 slides over to be a receiver for 3 in corner. 3 looks for his shot, a pass to 4, who is cutting, or a pass to 5, who is rolling to the blocks. Most often 3 will start a ball-man reversal by passing the ball out to 1.

1 must quickly reverse the ball to 4 on the backside with a direct pass or with a dribble penetration and then a pass to 4 or 2 posted inside the interior of the zone. On a dribble penetration the direct pass inside is often open as the defensive wing shifts up to guard 4 and leaves a hole in the interior of the defense behind him.

With the ball on top in 4's possession (see Diagram 8-17), the defense is forced to expand after being forced to contract. 4 is shaped up to shoot but looking inside to pass to 5, who is flashing, 2, who is on the blocks, or 3, who is on the baseline. 1 has moved into position to be a receiver for 4. 4 passes to 3 on the baseline and runs his

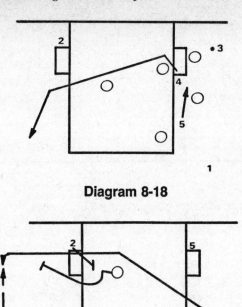

Diagram 8-18

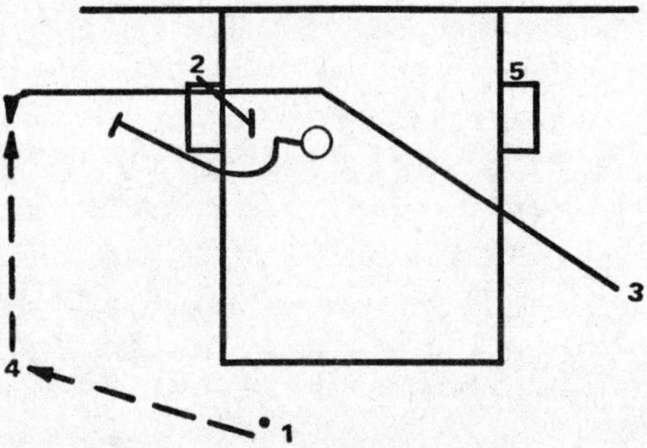

Diagram 8-19

diagonal cut to the blocks, pausing in a gap for a possible return pass.

Diagram 8-18 illustrates the ball position as 4 cuts to the baseline. 5 delays enough to allow 4 to clear the area before he cuts into the open area. 2 crosses opposite but can "X" back if an opening occurs on 5's cut. 4 must remember to be wide as he swings up to the free throw line on the backside of the zone. You have expanded, compressed, expanded, compressed, and expanded the zone again. This constant shifting creates gaps and errors.

One adjustment we like to use against the odd front and flex-match up zones is the use of screens, particularly on the baseline shifts of the interior defense. (See Diagram 8-19.) Against the 1-3-1 it is possible to screen the deep defender on the initial entry pass from 1 to 4. 2 screens for 3, who is crossing along the baseline. 2 must then step to the pocket as the bottom defender goes out to defend against 3.

The most effective screen occurs on the reversal of the ball to the

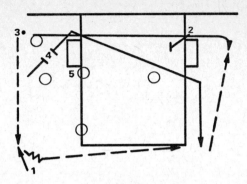

Diagram 8-20

backside of the zone. (See Diagram 8-20.) After passing the ball to 3, 4 runs his diagonal cut and comes up on the side of the lane to the free throw area. 3 starts the reversal by passing out to 1. Then 3 runs his baseline cut, rubbing off 2's screen on the backside of the zone. 5 runs his normal flash cut and roll. 1 quickly passes to 4, who has the same options as 5, 3, and 2. 4 is shaped up and ready to shoot, use a dribble penetration move, or pass to 5 flashing. He also has the option of passing to 2, who is on the blocks, or 3, who is coming off 2's screen.

The basic inside rotation series doesn't change much when it is played against perimeter zones. It matters very little whether the zone is a 2-3, 1-3-1, 1-2-2, or 2-1-2 zone.

Attacking the pressure zones requires very little adjustment to the basic inside rotation series. There are several options we add to the rotation series to take advantage of the opportunities afforded by this type of zone. Remember that our basic concept does not change, nor do the principal rotation routes of the players.

The odd front zones are most widely used by the pressure advocates. Not that you do not see the even fronts, such as 2-1-2 and 2-3, but the odd fronts afford more flexibility in pressuring your passing lanes. Thus, we will look at the 1-2-2 and 1-3-1 pressure zones to see how our inside power rotation series attacks them.

Against the 1-2-2 pressure zone (see Diagram 8-21) our initial set up is almost the same. The only difference is in our 1, 3, and 4 players. Since the perimeter players of the pressure zone line up in your passing lanes, our rule for 3 and 4 to be one stride higher automatically changes the depth of our alignment. When a defense attacks you out front with pressure, it is trying to create uncertainty in your players' passing and thus create turnovers.

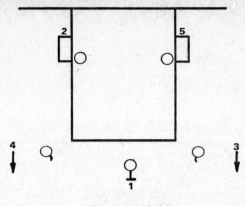

Diagram 8-21

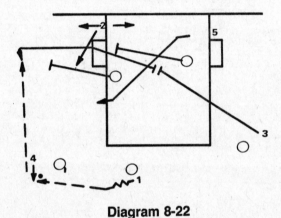

Diagram 8-22

You must remember, however, that the pressure applied in an extended area creates vulnerability somewhere else. The somewhere else is the interior. Stress this important point to your perimeter players, 3, 4, and especially 1, to be successful against pressure zones.

Because of this vulnerability, we, by design, want to extend the area some more. This is the reason for playing 3 and 4 one step higher than the defensive zone's perimeter players. By utilizing this rule, we can expand the defense beyond its ability to recover quickly enough to cover up defensive errors.

In Diagram 8-22, 1 has passed to 4, and 3 cuts to the baseline on the ball-side of the floor. 5 and 2 read and react. Our basic rotation series continues as before.

After passing to 3 on the baseline, 4 makes his diagonal cut. 4 must be sure to pause in the gap of the zone to allow 3 to see if 4 is

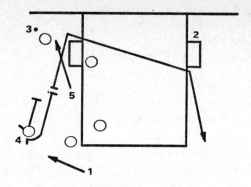

Diagram 8-23

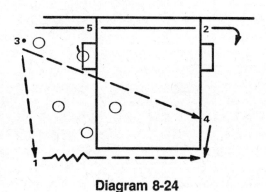

Diagram 8-24

open. (See Diagram 8-23.) If 3 is unable to pass inside to 4, who is cutting, or 5, who is rolling down the lane behind 4's cut, 3 starts the reversal of the ball. He may pass to 1 or skip pass directly to 4 on the backside of the zone. 3 then runs his baseline cut. (See Diagram 8-24.) In the event 3 cannot pass to 1 due to excellent defensive recovery and pressure or to 4 on a skip pass for the same reason, we use a post-stepout move. (See Diagram 8-25.) 5 steps out to be a receiver for 3's reversal pass. After receiving 3's pass, 5 immediately turns and looks inside for 2 flashing, 4 dropping down the lane, or 1 sliding to the pocket. 3 cuts to the open area on the baseline.

After passing to 2, 4, 3, or 1, 5 cuts to the blocks behind the interior defense ready to flash into the open area. Diagram 8-26 illustrates the players' moves as 2 receives 5's pass.

2 turns to face inside so he exerts maximum pressure on the

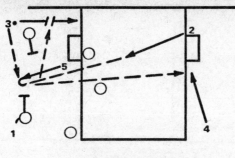

Diagram 8-25

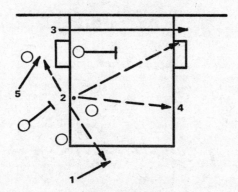

Diagram 8-26

interior defense as it adjusts. If he is open, 2 can shoot a short jumper; drive; pass to 3, who is crossing, 5, who is cutting to the blocks, or 4 on the backside; or make a vertical pass to 1 on the top.

At this juncture we are back in our basic inside rotation as illustrated in Diagrams 8-24 and 8-25. If 2 passes to 4 on the backside, 4 must be ready to shoot, pass, or drive. (See Diagram 8-27.)

On 4's pass to 3 on the baseline, 4 runs his diagonal cut to come up on the backside of zone. Remember that 4 must come up wider on this reversal. The zone has been compressed and now it should be expanded. Diagram 8-28 illustrates the basic rotation as it continues.

If 3 doesn't have a shot or an open area to pass to inside, 3 reverses the ball to 1 or skip passes to 4 on the backside.

Suppose the defense was superior in applying pressure to your perimeter players. Seeing this, 1 runs a dribble rotation (see Diagram 8-29). Whenever 1 drives at either wing, the 3 man in this instance, the

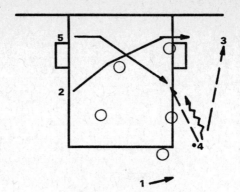

Diagram 8-27

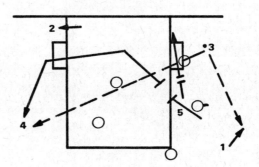

Diagram 8-28

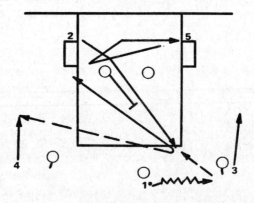

Diagram 8-29

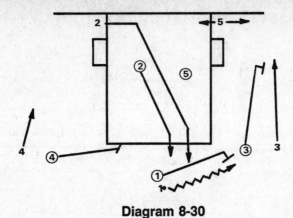

Diagram 8-30

wing must vacate. The offside post, in this case 2, flashes to the high post area. He must come as high as is necessary to be open for 1's pass—25 feet if necessary. Immediately upon receiving the pass, 2 turns to look inside to 5, who is crossing, or opposite to 4, who is sliding to the open area on the backside zone. 1 moves to the open area. After making his pass to 4, 2 rolls down the lane looking for an open area. 3 has moved to the open area opposite 4. If 2 passes to 4, 3 runs his baseline cut. If 2 passes to 3, 4 runs the baseline cut. Now we are in our basic inside power rotation series.

Anytime 1, 3, or 4 finds himself not guarded, he must use the penetration (pinch) move. Otherwise, the defense will have us outnumbered with no one on the ball. This creates a five-on-four situation for the defense. Thus, the penetration dribble is vital to your offense in these situations.

When it is played against the flex-match ups, our basic inside rotation series is adjusted only in that we screen more and use the dribble rotation as the entry into the offense.

Diagram 8-30 illustrates the dribble rotation against the flex-match up. As before, 1 drives straight at either 3 or 4, in this instance 3. 3 slides to the baseline, and 2 comes to the high post area and steps out for a pass from 1. 4 slides to the open area on the backside of zone.

5 crosses the lane as 2 receives 1's pass. (See Diagram 8-31.) 2 immediately looks inside to 5, who is crossing, and 4, who is in the offside pocket area. If 5 is not open, 2 passes to 4, who looks immediately inside to 5. 5 posts up as 4 receives 2's pass. If 5 is not open,

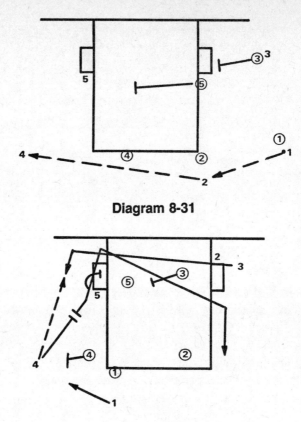

Diagram 8-31

Diagram 8-32

he screens for 3, who is crossing along the baseline. (See Diagram 8-32.) 4 passes to 3, who is coming off 5's baseline screen. 5 then posts up. After passing to 5 inside or 4 in the pocket, 2 rolls to the blocks opposite 5. Often, 2 is open for a skip pass; if not, he is in a position to rebound a shot by 4, 5, or 3.

The basic inside power rotation series is now in motion. (See Diagram 8-33.) After 4 passes to 3 on the baseline, he makes his diagonal cut to the blocks. He then continues up the lane on the backside. 3 reverses the ball to 1 or skip passes to 4 on the backside. 3 then crosses the baseline and rubs off 2's and 5's double screen. As 3 rubs off, 2 crosses to the backside of the zone for rebounding position.

Diagram 8-34 continues the inside rotation with the ball in 4's possession. 2 flashes to an open area of the interior. 4 can shoot, penetrate, or pass to 3, who is on the baseline, 2, who is flashing, or 5,

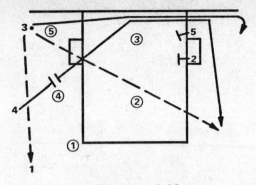

Diagram 8-33

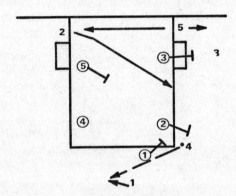

Diagram 8-34

who is posted up on the blocks. If 5 isn't open, he immediately crosses to the blocks opposite.

In previous sequences 4 has always passed inside to the post or to the baseline. When playing against the flex-match up, we like to reverse the ball on top occasionally. When this occurs, the rule changes for 3 and 4. 3 makes the baseline cut first, with 4 following. (See Diagram 8-35.) 4 slides to the open area on the backside and pauses to read the defensive slides. 5 screens for 3, who is running the baseline, and then posts up. 2 flashes into the gap of the interior of the zone. 1 can pass to 3, who is coming off 5's screen, or 2, who is flashing. Here 1 passes to 3 on the baseline. 3 should be shaped up and ready to shoot.

If 1 doesn't pass to 3 because of quick defensive adjustments, he should look immediately to 4, who is on the blocks behind the zone since defensive man 3 went with 2 flashing, leaving an open area

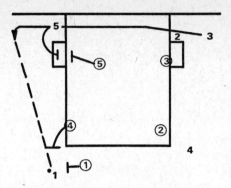

Diagram 8-35

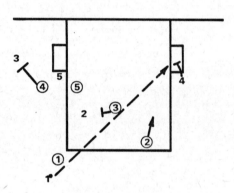

Diagram 8-36

behind him. 1 immediately lob passes to 4 behind the interior of the zone. (See Diagram 8-36.)

   In the event 4 is not open sliding behind the zone, he crosses the baseline rubbing off 2's screen. 3 swings up higher and wider to receive 1's pass. (See Diagram 8-37.) On receiving 1's pass, 3 looks to pass inside to 4, who is on the baseline coming off 2's screen. After passing to 4, 3 makes his diagonal cut, but in this instance he flattens it and crosses through middle of the zone to the open area on the backside.

   Diagram 8-38 illustrates 3's cut. If 4 does not have a shot and can't make a direct pass inside to 2 posted, he looks to skip pass to 3 on the backside or pass out to 1. 4 then runs his baseline cut. 3 has the option to shoot, drive, or pass to 5 or 4. We are now in our basic inside rotation movement, where 3 makes his diagonal cut to come up on the backside of the zone. Remember that 3 must rotate up wider. 2 flashes,

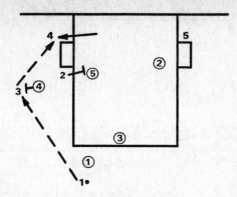

Diagram 8-37

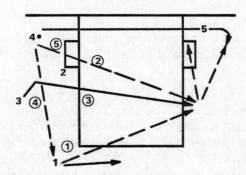

Diagram 8-38

while 4 crosses the baseline to be a receiver. 1 slides to the open area to be a receiver for 3's or 4's pass. (See Diagram 8-39.)

There are several important thoughts I want to emphasize to any coach trying to teach offense against zone defenses. Your point guard 1 has a tendency to be too deep as he reverses the ball. As the game wears on, 1 will have this tendency to overcome. For some reason, either from fear of a turnover or from concentrating so much on getting the ball to the open men, 1 develops this tendency. You cannot allow this to happen because he will lose his ability to penetrate the gap. Furthermore, when this happens 1 is not looking for his shot and has become just a ball returner. A good zone defense will seize upon this opportunity to play five men on four.

Your point guard must also watch for the direct pass inside to either post man, 2 or 5. Often, as the ball is being reversed to 1, or even as 1 is bringing the ball into the offensive forecourt, 1 can make

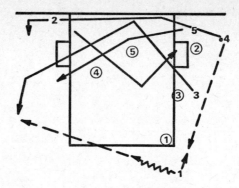

Diagram 8-39

this direct pass and should be encouraged to do so. Why? Because the perimeter players of the zone defense have become so conscious of ball reversal or getting to their assigned area that their initial shift is too quick. By anticipating this and using a ball fake, 1 can open the direct vertical pass inside.

One more important thought to remember: A pause is a valuable refresher for your cutters. All too often they will just cut through the gap and go on. When they hit that gap, they should slow down, pause, and be receivers. This will put an added burden on the interior zone defense, because once your cutter receives the ball in this position, the interior of the zone is vulnerable. You will have the defense outnumbered where it hurts them the most, in the interior.

What we have tried to emphasize is the importance of having your players develop an overall concept of why each of them is doing various things. They must know their roles as they fit into the whole team concept. They must know what we are trying to accomplish. Understanding of the strategic areas your offense must use to succeed—ball and man movement and penetration—is vital if you are to win.

Drill 8-1: 3 or 4 Penetration

Instructions: Use the same principles as in Drill 7-1. 1, 3, and 4 try to penetrate the defense, creating a two-on-one pinch move by defense. 1 dribble penetrates and passes to 3, who is stepping to the pocket. 4 has moved to the pocket on the opposite side of the zone. After passing to 3, 4 steps to open area to be available to 3 for a ball reversal. 3 can skip pass to 4 on the backside of the zone.

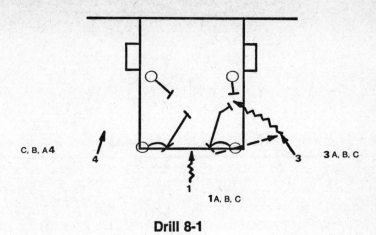

Drill 8-1

Teaching Points: You must stress to 1, 3, and 4 the importance of keeping their heads up so they can read the defense. In this drill you must emphasize to each player the importance of being shaped up and on balance when they receive a pass and of taking the dribble drive in strong when they are able to penetrate all the way. They must make sure passes are where the receiver can catch them on balance. Remind 1 not to play too deep and look just to reverse the ball.

Time Sequence: We work ten minutes early in the season. We work seven to five minutes in midseason. In the last third of the season five to three minutes is sufficient.

Practice Pressure: The offense must be successful four out of five times within a 60 second time span. The offense must use a minimum of three passes each time. If a turnover or a mistake occurs or time runs out, the defense wins. The winner gains bonus points, and the loser runs. The defense runs transition game on all turnovers.

Drill 8-2: 3 on 4 Rotation

Instructions: This drill is similar to Drill 7-2. Wings 3 and 4 pass and cut diagonally, making sure to pause on their cut. They must look for the opening and head for it. The passer, 1, 3, or 4, must read the movement of the defense. The 1 man, as well as 3 and 4, must be taught to read the defensive moves before they receive a pass while they're on the perimeter. All three players should

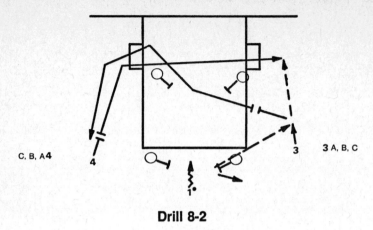

Drill 8-2

utilize the penetration move. Either 3 or 4 may skip pass to the backside at any time. Rotate in new offensive players as desired. Your 5 and 2 play defense versus 1, 3, and 4.

Teaching Points: 3 and 4 must step to the gap as 1 penetrates. The offside wing should pause for a possible skip pass from the opposite wing before cutting through zone. Remind each player to be shaped up to receive the pass and on balance to shoot or pass. After receiving 1's pass, 3 passes to 4 in the corner. 3 must cut and pause in the gap for a possible return pass. 1 must slide to the open area to be a receiver of 4's pass. 4 runs the baseline but should be alert to the defense overshifting or shifting too quickly. If the defense overshifts or shifts too quickly, 4 slips up to pocket vacated by 3's pass and cut. We want each player to use the bounce pass, overhead pass, and ball fakes whenever possible.

Time Sequence: We work ten minutes early in the season. We work seven minutes in midseason and five minutes in late season.

Practice Pressure: Players must complete three, five, or seven straight passes with no mistakes or the offense must score three out of four times. Sometimes we combine the two methods. Sometimes we place a time limit for the offense to score or complete a designated number of passes. If the defense succeeds in preventing the offense from being successful, they win. Losers run, and winners receive bonus points.

Drill 8-3: 2 on 4 Post Rotate

Instructions: 1, 3, and 4 can only penetrate the reverse ball by skip

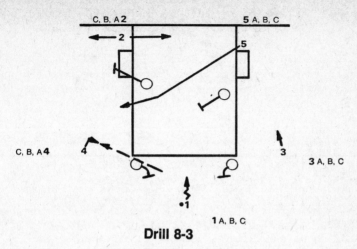

Drill 8-3

passing or a normal reversal. They may not shoot or run their (3 and 4) diagonal cuts. 5 and 2 are working on their inside rotation moves here. Rotate in new players as desired. This drill is also run against a 1-2-1 set to give players an odd front to work against.

Teaching Points: Our perimeter people must work on their ability to read and react to the defensive shifts. Making the correct pass in a given situation is vital. 5 and 2 must work on their timing of cuts and coordination of movement together. What is critically important here is for 5 and 2 to receive the ball at the proper moment, which is when they are just getting open. It is important that 1, 3, and 4 learn to make this critical direct pass inside. They must develop confidence in their ability to make their offensive moves without putting the ball on the floor.

Time Sequence: We work ten minutes early in the season. We work five minutes in midseason and three minutes late in the season.

Practice Pressure: The ball must penetrate inside on every third, sixth, or ninth pass. If 5 and 2 don't have a shot, they must kick the ball back out to the opposite side the pass came in from. 5 or 2 must score two out of every three times they handle the ball. If the defense succeeds in preventing either offensive movement—a shot or a pass—two times, they win. At this point the transition game is added. Any turnover scores two points. We play a ten-point game in this situation. The offense gets two points and the ball for each basket scored. The offense also gets a point for every direct pass successfully completed inside that results in a score. Losers run.

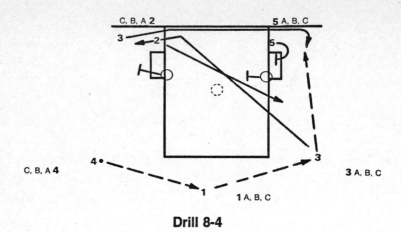

Drill 8-4

Drill 8-4: Baseline Screens

Instructions: 5 and 2 work on their rotation moves but must screen for the baseline cutter. 3 runs the baseline to cut off 2's baseline screen. 1 is at the point, 4 is on the left wing, and another 3 man plays the normal 3 position. The second 3 man, after passing to the baseline, runs a diagonal cut. The baseline 3 either shoots or reverses the ball to 1. On the ball reversal the baseline 3 steps out and the next 3 man takes his position at the wing. Meanwhile, 1 has reversed the ball to 4, and 4 has passed to the second 3 man on baseline, who is coming off 2's screen. Later we change the drill to the opposite side of the floor, and 4 runs the baseline with a second 4 man. We start the drill with two interior defensive players and add a third defensive player later.

Teaching Points: 5 and 2 must work together to get open at precisely the right moment. What is important is that 2 and 5 set a good road block screen. 3 must come off the screen, plant his inside foot, and be squared up to receive pass and ready to shoot. What you must teach 5 and 2 is to screen an area the defense will shift into as they shift to meet this new attack.

Time Sequence: We work ten minutes early in the season. Later we cut the time to five minutes. Late in the season we reduce the time to three to two minutes.

Practice Pressure: 5 and 2 must set a proper screen three out of four times. The defense must defeat the screen twice and put pressure on the shooter.

9

Adding the

Inside Power Control Game

The inside power control game is a vital adjunct to your offense as the game is played today. As the need to control the tempo of the game becomes more critical due to foul trouble, theirs or yours, loss of momentum, lack of speed by your team, or a multitude of other reasons, it behooves one to have another means of keeping control of the game.

The type of control that has made the greatest impact on the game of basketball in its present form is probably the four-corner offense, as popularized by the University of North Carolina and its outstanding coach Dean Smith. Coach Smith's four-corner offense has added new dimensions to offense and problems for coaches trying to defend against this type of attack.

We have had ample opportunity to view the success of the four-corner offense year in and year out in the A.C.C., so it was only natural that we adapt it to fit our needs. Over the years we have refined our version of this fine inside control game.

Whereas North Carolina uses basically one super player to control the ball and pass inside or penetrate the middle while the other four players remain somewhat stationary, we have decided to involve all five players in our movement. This is not to say that we disagree with Coach Smith's principles, but this method is better suited to our needs. There is nothing really new in basketball, just continual changes and adjustments to what has already been tried and proven successful.

The four-corner offense as we run it has been adjusted to fit our needs at the high school level, though I feel it could be used successfully at any level. One of the reasons we use five-man movement is floor space. In high school basketball the court is 84 feet long, while in college basketball the court is 94 feet long. We felt our smaller area afforded the defense several advantages. One of them is that there is less floor space to cover. Another is that there are better double team possibilities. A third is that with the defense more compressed the penetration dribble is much more difficult to execute by your middle man.

Some coaches will question the wisdom of having all of the offensive players involved in the movement, especially the middle or hub of the offense. To allow your big men to operate in this highly sensitive area would seem rather foolish, like inviting instant disaster. But let me remind you that the opposing big man is more often than not a defensive liability when you are playing against the four-corner offense because of the greater area that must be covered and the inherent one-on-one problems.

BASIC FLOOR BALANCE

We send our post men 5 and 2 to the endline corners. 1 is generally in the middle, and 3 and 4 are in the mid-court corners. (See Diagram 9-1.) Any one of our perimeter players could start as the middle man. Which player takes this initial area to start the offense is often determined by the ball handling abilities of the players.

BASIC MOVEMENT

The basic movement is initiated by the middle man's (1) penetration to the free throw line area. At this point the defense is forced to give help to stop 1's penetration move. (See Diagram 9-2.) At this juncture 1 can pass out to either 4 or 3. After passing out to 4 or 3, 1 goes to the blocks on the side he passed to. He does this to clear the middle for the player (3 or 4) he passed to.

Diagram 9-3 illustrates how we fill the area 4 vacates as he dribble penetrates into the middle. The corner man, 2 in this case, slides up the sideline to fill the spot vacated by 4. 1 slides over to fill the open area in the baseline corner, which was vacated by 2.

This basic movement can be continued to the opposite side of

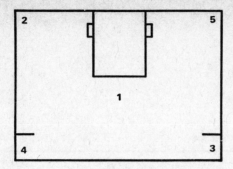

Diagram 9-1

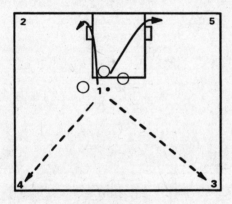

Diagram 9-2

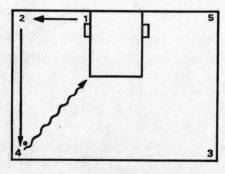

Diagram 9-3

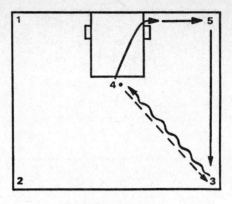

Diagram 9-4

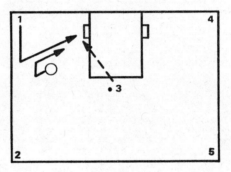

Diagram 9-5

floor. (See Diagram 9-4.) After penetrating, 4 passes out to 3 and cuts to the blocks to the side he passes to. 3 now penetrates into the middle, looking to drive for a layup or pivot and pass back outside to either 2 or 5.

Your baseline corner players must always be alert to what their own defensive men are doing. For example, when your baseline corner player slides up the sideline, he reads his defensive player's position. When he sees his man turn his head or try to help out as he starts up the sideline, he reverses and cuts hard to the basket, looking for a bounce pass and a layup. This move is only attempted while the ball is in the hands of the middle man. (See Diagram 9-5.) 1 starts up the sideline and, realizing his man is not paying close attention to him, reverses hard and fast to the blocks. 3 should bounce pass to 1, leading him to the basket. Why is this move available? Mainly because the defense gets too used to the basic movement and relaxes. At this precise moment the defense is vulnerable to a quick hard reversal by the cutter. If 1 isn't open on this cut, he returns to the corner.

To have a successful control game, the defense must be constantly exploited. This offensive set is run to attack and score, not to hold the ball and run the clock. Although we do run time off the clock if it is important to our game strategy, this is not the primary reason for using this spread attack. It simply is a different method to be used in scoring.

As mentioned earlier in this chapter, fouls play a great part in the outcome of any game. Sometimes, to our chagrin, too much so. To me it is foolhardy to continue playing at your normal tempo when your opponent is shooting one plus one; for example, when you are three fouls away from being into the bonus situation.

I have seen too many games where leads evaporated, control of the game dissipated, and the game was eventually lost. But what if we can protect this lead while still attacking and force the other team to foul? What if they choose not to see us run the clock out? What are they to do but come out after the ball? Then, when the fouls even up, we may go back to our normal tempo.

BACK-DOOR CUT

After moving the defense in and out several times, the corner baseline player opposite the ball can flash to the post area. (See Diagram 9-6.) As 2 flashes, 3 makes the diagonal pass to 2. 2 comes as high as he must to receive the pass. The instant the ball touches 2's hands, 4 cuts hard to the blocks, looking for 2's bounce pass. After passing into 2, 3 crosses to the opposite corner for floor balance. 5 has come to the foul line extended area on 2's flash. He now goes on to fill 3's vacated area. 1 clears to the corner to fill the area left open by 1's movement.

This option can be run to either side of the floor. There are times when, due to our opponent's method of defending against our attack, we will flash a guard and back-door cut one of our post men. There are times when a mismatch is available to your team due to size, speed, quickness, or lack of quickness that your team can take advantage of.

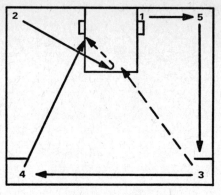

Diagram 9-6

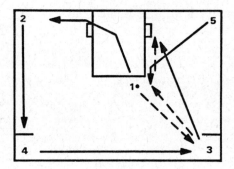

Diagram 9-7

BALL-SIDE CUT

Our ball-side cut is just that, a back-door cut coming from the ball-side. (See Diagram 9-7.) Player movement is not changed. The basic rotation of the ball and players remains the same. The option is keyed by calling the number of the player who is to flash into the post area. In this instance 5 flashes on the ball-side. 3 passes into 5 and cuts hard and fast to the basket. 5 bounce passes to 3, leading him to the basket. 1, who had passed out to 3, has cleared to the baseline opposite the ball. 2 should rotate up to fill the area vacated when 4 rotated to fill the area opened by 3's back-door cut.

There are times when 3 runs his back-door cut that his clearing the area will open up a drive by 5. If the defensive player guarding 3 keeps good coverage, 5 will have an open side of the floor to go one-on-one. (See Diagram 9-8.) This option is frequently available, but if 5 isn't

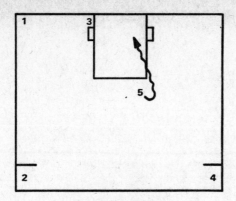

Diagram 9-8

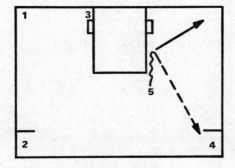

Diagram 9-9

able to drive, he should pass out to 2 or 4 in the mid-court corners. His rule is to fill the open area, which happens to be the same area he flashed from. In this instance there is no rotation. (See Diagram 9-9.)

The normal rotation resumes as 4 penetrates to the middle and 5 slides up to fill the space vacated by 4. (See Diagram 9-10.) 3, who is on the blocks, has the option of holding or crossing to the blocks opposite. This option is used as 3 reads and reacts to his defensive man's reactions to 4's penetration dribble. 4 can pass off to 3 if 3's defensive man tries to help out or continue his drive to the basket.

REBOUNDING ASSIGNMENTS

With the spread formation rebounding is at a premium. This is the one risk you must face up to when employing this offense.

Stress the need to crash the offensive boards aggressively. We

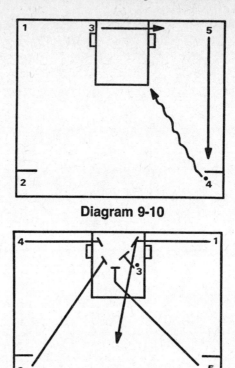

Diagram 9-10

Diagram 9-11

insist on taking only the high percentage shot when we are in the spread formation to help offset the rebounding problem.

Diagram 9-11 illustrates the rebounding assignments we adhere to in our four-corner control system. The principle rules remain the same. The only change is who rebounds inside on the blocks. With the player movement involved in the four-corner offense, it is obvious that there are times our post men will be caught outside. But this is not as bad a problem as it would appear to be. Remember, their big men are caught outside too.

The two baseline corner players, in this instance 1 and 4, rebound on the blocks. The shooter, 3, rebounds on the line of 45° ball-side. The outside corner player, 2, who is off the ball, rebounds on the line of 45°. 5, being ball-side, rebounds down the gut. No matter where 1 is, his responsibility is still to be deep safety after checking his rebounding assignment. Occasionally, we have adjusted our assignments and kept both outside corner players back as safeties.

TRANSITION ASSIGNMENTS

Even if you take only the high percentage shot, once it is taken you are in the twilight zone between offense and defense. Go after the second and third shots. Once the battle of the boards is lost, you are in the transition game.

Your players must react to the change from offense to defense mentally as well as physically. This is phase one of our transition. The second phase is the actual transition to your defensive perimeter. The perimeter could be full court, three-quarter court, or half court defense.

Diagram 9-12 depicts our rules for the transition from offense to defense. The rules for our players in transition remain the same. The numbered players in the circles are our offensive players shown as moving to defense since we are now considering ourselves on defense.

Since 5's man secured the rebound, it is 5's rule to jam the rebounder. He then runs a streak pattern to the blocks opposite the ball-side. 2, being the off rebounder, crosses through the nearest mid-court passing lane, since we want to run through their passing lanes. 1 heads up court to be as deep as their deepest player. 4 rebounds the help-side position on the line of 45° and then crosses through their rebounders' outlet area. He should hesitate and run to the next deepest receiver and then to the middle of the lane. 3 crosses the rebounders' outlet passing lane, heading to the deepest receiver opposite the re-

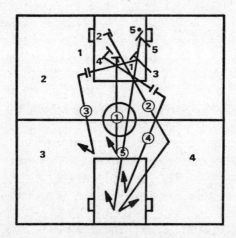

Diagram 9-12

bounder. 3 then heads to the foul line area, picking up the nearest open man.

Whenever a player enters an open man area—one with no opposing player—his rule is to cross back through the next passing lane and find the next nearest open receiver while continuing down court.

PRACTICE DRILLS
FOR OUR INSIDE CONTROL GAME

Practice drills help develop the ability to respond automatically to each situation as it occurs. Therefore, we practice with great concentration and intensity in each drill.

Drill 9-1: Back-Door Cut

Instructions: We place 2 and 5 in the baseline corners. 4 and 3 are in the left midcourt corner. 1 has a second ball. 1, 3, and 4 are in midcourt corners. The drill starts with 2 flashing and 3 passing to 2. As the pass to 2 is made, 4 runs a hard, fast back-door cut. 3 then clears to the left vacated corner to fill the open area as he would on regular back-door cut and to the end of line. 1A has a second ball; 5 flashes to the post. 1A passes to 5, fills the opposite corner, and goes to the end of the line. 4A, who is next in line, cuts back door. The post rebounds the shooter's shot, passes to the mid-corner, and goes to the opposite baseline corner. Add defense to 2, 5, 4, and 3 as the players develop timing and improve their skills.

Teaching Points: The baseline corner player who comes to meet the pass must be at the proper angle to receive the ball. He must be on balance when catching the ball. Then he must pivot to face the basket and use the correct pass at the proper angle. The mid-court corner players must be reminded not to put the ball on the floor until the defensive player is six feet from them. The five-second count does not begin until then. They must make the correct pass into the flash post. The pass must be accurate to enable the flash post to receive it on balance. The mid-court cutter must jab step and then cut hard and fast to the blocks. But he must remain under control as he receives the post man's pass. He should be sure to sight in on his shooting target before he goes up for the layup.

Time Sequence: Early in the season we work six minutes. The time is

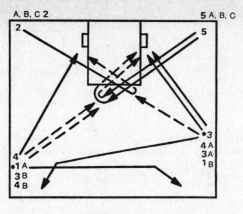

Drill 9-1

later cut to four minutes. Late in the season we work only two minutes.

Practice Pressure: Without the defense, the players are allowed no mistakes in this drill. That means the entire team for however long the drill is run or for a specific number of times run. When the defense has been added, the offense must be successful two out of three, three out of four, or four our of six times. Losers run as many sprints as drills they lost.

Drill 9-2: Ball-Side Cut

Instructions: 2 and 5 are in the baseline corners, and 1, 3, and 4 are in the mid-court corners. This drill requires two balls. We start with 3 on the right side. 5 flashes, and, as he posts up, 3 passes to 5. 3 then cuts to the blocks looking for a return pass. 5 rebounds 3's shot and passes back to 1B in the same line 3 started from. 5 then goes to the opposite baseline corner. 3 continues to the rear of the opposite line in the mid-court corner. As 3 clears, 4 passes to 2, who is posting, and cuts hard to the blocks, looking for a return pass. The same procedure is repeated by 4 and 2. 2 rebounds 4's shot and passes back to same line. 4 clears to the end of line at the opposite mid-court corner. Add defense to each corner. The offense rotates to defense after each series.

Teaching Points: It is important for your players posting up to be shaped up and ready to receive a pass. Make sure they are on balance, with their knees flexed and their target hands in position to receive the pass. After catching the ball, they must keep it

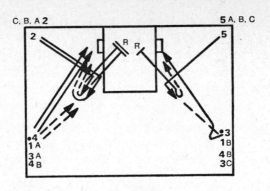

Drill 9-2

close to the body between the shoulder and the chin. This prevents the defensive man from slapping the ball away. It also helps offensive fakes and passing. The passer, 1, 3, or 4, plants his outside foot and cuts hard to the blocks. He must cut hard but under control and be on balance and ready to receive the pass and shoot.

Time Sequence: We work five minutes early in the season. In mid-season we work three minutes. Late in the season we work two minutes.

Practice Pressure: Without defense, the offense is allowed no mistakes in passing, cutting, or shooting. When defense is used, the offense is not allowed to miss a layup. Bonus points are awarded to the defense if they can force a mistake. The offense also receives bonus points for success. Losers stay at their positions until they succeed, at which time we total up their pluses and minuses to see if they run or receive bonus points.

Drill 9-3: Situation

Instructions: We run our inside rotation either five on zero or five on five. With or without defense we are working on basic movements and timing. The middle man (1) penetrates and passes out to 4. 1 clears to the blocks on the side he passes to. 4 penetrates the middle. Our basic pattern of play continues as a new player becomes the middle man.

Teaching Points: The middle man must dribble penetrate with his head up. He must see what the defense is doing at all times and always be alert to the double team situation. Floor balance is vital

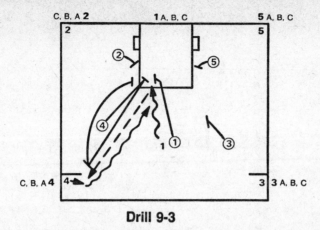

Drill 9-3

and must be maintained. Be sure your players stay in the corners. They must use the maximum floor space. Be sure to emphasize to your players not to put the ball on the floor until the defensive man is within six feet of them. Keep reminding your players to take only the layup. Teaching patience will be your most difficult task.

Time Sequence: Early in the season we work for eight minutes. In the middle of the season we cut the time to five minutes. Late in the season we reduce the time to three minutes.

Practice Pressure: We apply pressure in this drill several ways. The first method is to play a ten-point game. The team, offense or defense, that scores ten points wins. Losers must run. The offense is awarded two points for each basket they score, and they get to keep the ball. For every minute, minute and a half, or two minutes with no turnovers, the offense is awarded one point. All this is kept on the scoreboard, which is used daily during practice. The defense is awarded one point for every turnover, two points for a successful completion of a fastbreak, and one point for each time the offense is prevented from holding onto the ball with no mistakes for one minute. Each successful rebound gains one point for the offense or defense. Players and managers not involved must select which team they believe will win. If they choose wrong, they run with the losers. The other method we use involves setting a score and a time sequential on the scoreboard; for example, there are three minutes left in the game and we are leading by three points. The offensive players must hold this lead or improve upon it. If they lose, they run.

10

The Transition Game

In today's fast-paced society we would be remiss if we failed to include the fastbreak in our offensive system. The players have always enjoyed a run-and-gun show as much as the fans. I like to run, but the running is going to be disciplined and under control.

To my way of thinking a fastbreak is beautiful to behold. Crisp passing delivered precisely to players running at top speed is like poetry in motion. But this poetry in motion is generally confined to the stereotyped three-on-two, three-on-one, and two-on-one fastbreak systems. True, these are what a team should strive for, and we do, but must a fastbreak be confined to just these systems? I don't think so. But how many times have you witnessed a team pull out and wait for the opposing team to get in position once their initial fastbreak thrust was nullified by the defense. Why not carry your break all the way through right into your offense? More teams are succeeding in this area all the time.

In this way the fastbreak becomes an integral part of the transition game. Thus, the transition game begins with the rebound, turnover, or made shot and ends with your team moving into your offense without stopping to set up. A five-on-five situation is still a transition break.

One of the finest exponents of this style is Sonny Allen at Southern Methodist University. Coach Allen helped reshape my thinking in this area. His main thought is to individualize each player's assignment. We have used this approach in our system. It has helped us cut down on our turnovers. With ideas picked up through other coaches and watching teams, we have evolved a system that fits into our philosophy of play.

ADVANTAGES OF THE
NUMBERED TRANSITION BREAK

By numbering our fastbreak we have maintained the basic pattern of play throughout our entire offensive system. The 1 man is our primary outlet receiver. We release our 3 and 4 men to fly to the shooting spots on the line of 45°, but only after we have secured the rebound. Our primary rebounders are 2 and 5. After securing the rebound, 2 becomes the trailer on the left. 5 is the safety and the trailer to the left of 1.

The advantages of this system stem from the simplicity of each player's responsibilities. Each player has a definite role to fill. Your best shooters, 3 and 4, will be taking the shots you want from where they practice them and in their range. They don't have to handle the ball, so they are able to run a streak pattern to the shooting spots. If they can obtain consistent open shots, their shooting percentages will show a marked improvement.

Turnovers are minimized by placing the burden of advancing the ball on the shoulders of one player, the point guard. Instead of teaching all of your players, you are able to concentrate your energies on only your point guards. This reduces the amount of teaching time. Facilitating your teaching is always of utmost importance. Specialization of your player's assignments has to augment whatever system you choose to use.

Entering into your offense directly from a five-on-five transition break is a tremendous advantage to your team. The defense is most vulnerable at the moment they have all five players back but the players are still adjusting to find the men they are guarding. In the case of a zone defense, they will not have been able to fill the area they are assigned to guard yet. It is at this moment, when you should be taking advantage of this defensive weakness, that many teams will pull out and set up to start their offense. If you do this you are missing an opportunity to search and destroy while the defense is searching to find you.

RULES FOR THE EXECUTION OF THE FASTBREAK

We start with your most important player, the 1 man. The point guard must be taught how to get open. We prefer the middle of the lane for our 1 man to operate in. (See Diagram 10-1.) If 1 isn't open in the

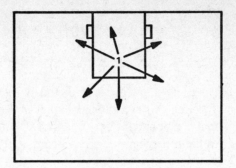

Diagram 10-1

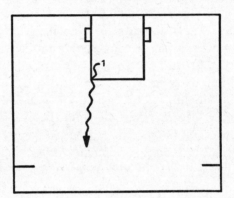

Diagram 10-2

middle, he must move to an area that is open to receive the outlet pass. 1 should take a quick look down court before he makes his move to get open. If he has time to do this he will be able to ascertain what passing lanes are open, if any, so that he can make a quicker release of his pass to the open receiver.

The 1 man's responsibilities are then to push the ball up the floor as quickly as possible via the dribble. 1 heads for the foul line on the right side. (See Diagram 10-2.) As 1 is pushing the ball up the floor, if 3 or 4 becomes open, 1 may elect to pass off to either one of them. His decision is determined by the capabilities of either 3 or 4. Can 3 or 4 put the ball on the floor well? Do they know their shooting range? Maybe they would be required to pass, and we do not consider one of them to be a very good passer on the break. 1 must know the capabilities of each of his teammates and play to them.

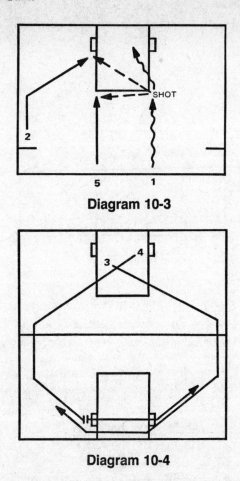

Diagram 10-3

Diagram 10-4

As 1 approaches the area of the foul line, he must make a split-second decision as to whether he should penetrate all the way, pull up and take his jumper, pass to 2, who is trailing on his left at the sideline, or pass to 5, who is trailing to his left at the foul line area. (See Diagram 10-3.)

Our 3 and 4 players are to run a streak pattern until they reach the foul line extended area. They are to run as wide as possible and, when they reach the foul line area, plant their outside feet and cut sharply for the blocks on the line of 45°.

Our 3 man always runs the left side while the 4 man runs the right side. We cross under the basket, with 4 pausing to screen for 3. In this way they end up in their normal offensive positions. (See Diagram

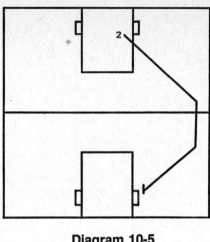

Diagram 10-5

10-4.) It is important to note that 3 and 4 will always fill the left and right sides respectively no matter where they are on the floor defensively. Also, after crossing the lane they are to come out on the line of 45°.

After rebounding, the 2 man heads up the left side trailing the 3 man by about ten feet. (See Diagram 10-5.) It is important to keep this distance because as 3 crosses the defensive man usually flows with him. This creates a vacant space behind 3. 1 knows this and should always be alert to it. If 2 doesn't receive a pass, he stops on the blocks, setting a screen for 4, who is crossing under.

5 is responsible for inbounding the ball to 1 after all made baskets or deep to 3 and 4, who are streaking, if they are open and we want this pass. He is the safety man and trails 1 up the floor. 5 should trail 1 by about twelve to fifteen feet. (See Diagram 10-6.) What 5 must be constantly aware of is the situation ahead of him. If 1 passes to 3 or 4, who are streaking, 5 must turn on the juice and crash the offensive boards as soon as he recognizes that a shot is about to be taken.

If 1 has pushed the ball up the floor via the dribble and reached the foul line area, 5 approaches the head of the circle looking for 1's pass. 5 can either shoot the jumper or penetrate to the basket for a layup. If 1 passes to 3, who is coming off 4's screen, 5 angles to the blocks looking for 3's direct pass inside to him on the blocks.

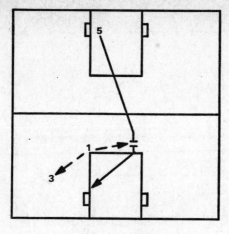

Diagram 10-6

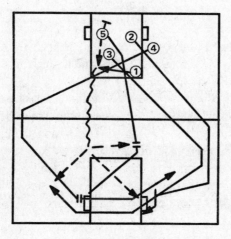

Diagram 10-7

INITIATING THE TRANSITION BREAK

To my way of thinking the most dynamic transition break is off the defensive rebound and outlet pass when run to perfection. Diagram 10-7 illustrates just how the players carry out their responsibilities.

Once it is certain we have secured the rebound, 3 and 4 release on their streak pattern. 3 heads up the left side, always looking for and

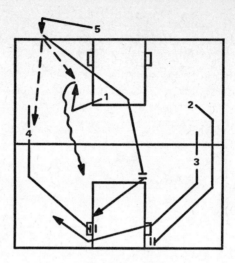

Diagram 10-8

expecting 1's pass. If 3 doesn't receive 1's pass in his shooting spot, he cuts on the line of 45°, crossing under, and comes out off 4's screen on the line of 45°.

4 releases up the right side looking for 1's pass and, failing to get one as he reaches his shooting spot cuts on the line of 45° to the blocks. Here he pauses to screen for 3, who is crossing. Then he releases to come out on the line of 45° off 2's screen.

1 moves quickly to get open. After catching 5's outlet pass, 1 should turn and look up court to see if 3 and 4 are open before *he puts the ball on the floor*. More open men are missed just because the 1 man puts the ball on the floor before he looks up court. Seeing no one open, 1 pushes the ball up court as quickly as possible but under control. Upon reaching the foul line area, 1 must decide whether to pass to 3, 5, or 2, penetrate, or shoot. His responsibilities are immense and the decisions must be made in seconds, but it is better that only one player make the decision than five.

2 heads up the left side trailing 3. When 2 sees 3 cross, he cuts hard on the line of 45° to the blocks. He must be alert for a pass. If he doesn't receive one, 2 screens on the blocks for 4, who is crossing.

5 trails 1 as he pushes the ball up the floor. Remember, 5 must know what is happening up the floor. When he recognizes the possibility of a shot, he is no longer a trailer but an aggressive rebounder. As long as 1 has the ball, he follows behind and to the left of 1. As 1 enters

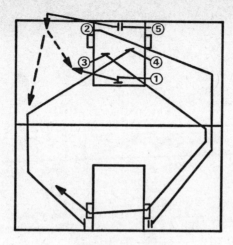

Diagram 10-9

the foul line area, 5 prepares to receive 1's pass for a jumper or a drive. If 1 passes to 3, 5 angles to the blocks.

Even if your opponent scored, you have a chance for the transition break, although this is not the preferred way to run. We have 5 take the ball out of bounds. (See Diagram 10-8.) 5 must take the ball out of the net and gain depth along the baseline as he runs to the right sideline. 5 looks deep to 4 or 3, who are streaking up the court, and then in to 1. 1 turns and looks immediately down court at 4 and 3 before he puts the ball on the floor. 2 trails 3 on the left, and 5 trails 1 up the middle. The same options are available as before. 1 can pass off to 4, 3, 2, or 5.

The free throw attempt is another method of making the transition break. (See Diagram 10-9.) We will look at this situation from the made shot. 5 always lines up on the right side, with 2 opposite on the left. 4 lines up on the right side opposite 3. 1 takes the top position and is responsible for blocking out their shooter at the foul line. As the ball descends through the net, 5 takes it and runs out of bounds, increasing his angle while looking deep. He then throws to 1. 3 and 4 check off their man and then cross and run a streak pattern for the shooting spots. 2 trails left, and 5 follows to the left behind 1. The same options are available to 1 as before. He can pass to 4, 3, 2, or 5 or look for his own shot, either a jumper or a penetration drive.

Rebounding a missed foul shot would be the same as rebounding a

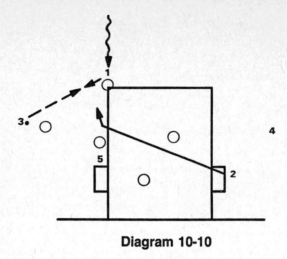

Diagram 10-10

missed field goal. The only difference is the advantage of being afforded a stationary inside position.

COMPLETION OF THE TRANSITION BREAK

The initial break will not always succeed. What follows is the
transition into our offense from the five-on-five situation. After running through the first options, we are now in the situation shown in
Diagram 10-10.

The ball is in the possesion of 3, who looks inside to feed 5, who
is cutting to the blocks. If 5 is not open, 3 return passes to 1 after
exhausting his possibilities. As the ball reaches 1, 2 flashes to the high
post. As this happens, 1 can pass inside to 2. If 2 receives the pass
immediately, 4 cuts back door, looking for a pass from 2. If 2 isn't
open, 1 will immediately run whatever option he feels will work. 1
could run the 3, 4, 5, 2, or 1 play. In some instances we will designate
what option is to be run in a particular game.

Developing the necessary skills one must have to fastbreak takes
repeated drilling. Like anything else, one must practice this phase of
basketball the same as all other phases. You must repeat the fundamentals over and over. They must be practiced with intensity. When these
two elements are combined, the players will remember the fundamentals and develop an ability to cope with pressure situations.

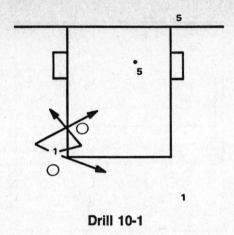

Drill 10-1

Drill 10-1: Outlet Pass to 1 Man

Instructions: Your post men are the rebounders. They toss the ball off the backboard, catch it, turn, and throw the outlet pass to 1. 1 starts in the area of the foul line and is double teamed front and back. 1 must move to get open as soon as the ball is tossed off the glass. Rotate in new players as desired. Add a defensive player to your rebounder later in the drill.

Teaching Points: Have your rebounder snatch the rebound with two hands and come down in a spread-eagle position. Under pressure we want our rebounder to turn away. He will have a clear outlet pass in the opposite direction. His pass must be crisp and on the money. You must teach 1 to read the defensive pressure on himself as well as that on the rebounder. 1 has to use head and shoulder fakes along with sharp angle cuts to get open. Be sure to emphasize to 1 that after receiving the outlet pass he must turn and look up the court before *putting the ball* on the floor.

Time Sequence: Early in the season we work five minutes. In midseason the time is reduced to three minutes. In late season we spend one minute.

Practice Pressure: We allow 1 only three seconds to get open from the moment 5 touches the ball on the rebound. 5 must make the correct outlet pass to 1. Bonus points are awarded for a successful completion.

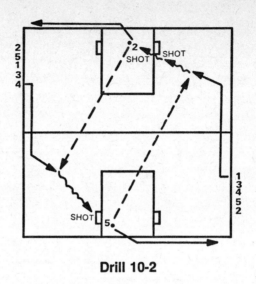

Drill 10-2

Drill 10-2: Two-Ball Outlet Pass

Instructions: This drill starts with a rebounder in possession of a ball at each basket. The rebounders toss the ball off the glass. As this action occurs, the first man in each line breaks down court looking for the outlet pass. After throwing his outlet pass, the rebounder goes to tne end of the outlet receiving line. In this drill we designate whether receivers are to shoot layup or pull up for the jump shot. They rebound their own shots and outlet the next pass. Then they follow their rule and go to the end of the line. During the course of the drill, the length of the outlet pass is made from any point from mid-court to the blocks. The drill is switched to left side of the floor and run the same way, but on this side everything is done left-handed, from making the outlet pass to shooting—except the jump shot.

Teaching Points: The rebounder must pivot and throw an accurate outlet pass with as much velocity as necessary. On the long pass we want the ball to be arched and the receiver to run under it. The ball will bounce to a height in direct proportion to its descending arch. Why is this important? I'll answer this with another question. How many times have you watched a receiver wide open be missed because the pass was too long and too fast? Probably all too often if you have witnessed very many games. The receiver must run a streak pattern until he reaches the foul line extended

area, where he plants his outside foot and cuts on the line of 45°
to the blocks. All the time he is looking for the pass. Be sure to
tell each shooter to go up under control with his head up looking
at his shooting target. When going at a fast pace for a shot, most
players have a tendency to bring their head up as they shoot. This
will only lead to ulcers for you.

Time Sequence: We work ten minutes early in the season. By midseason the time has been cut to six minutes. In late season we
reduce the time to four minutes.

Practice Pressure: The first method of putting pressure on the players
is to establish how many layups they must make in a row, for
example, 20. We also put a time limit on it, such as 20 in two
minutes. Another time we will count the number of mistakes in
each two-minute segment. This means we would run five two-
minute segments. To make fewer mistakes than allowed on four
out of five tries is considered successful. To fail is to run out
drills. The entire team runs.

Drill 10-3: Three-on-Two Continuous Transition Break

Instructions: All 1 men are at the mid-court line. We place all 2 and 5
men out of bounds under one basket and the 3 and 4 men out of
bounds under the other basket. Any of your players may start out
on defense. They are in a tandem position. A player starts the
drill as 1 man, with a 3 and 4 at mid-court. They attack in either
direction, in this instance against defenders (5) and (3). As soon
as (5) and (3) secure the ball via a missed or made shot, 1, who is
at mid-court, steps in to receive the outlet pass from either (5) or
(3). If the ball is secured from a made shot, (5) would inbound it.
(5) and (3) then join 1 in a three-on-two, transition break in the
opposite direction. 5 fills his trailer role while 3 runs a streak
pattern on the left side. This procedure is continued with (4) and
(2) joining a new 1 man. (2) trails on the left side, with 4 streaking the right side. After each break, two new defenders step in,
while the offense steps out of bounds on the baseline. The 1 man
goes to the end of the line at mid-court.

Teaching Points: Have each player fill his lanes properly. This is
where the action is fast and constant. This is also where you must
harden your 1 man. His ability to recognize situations and make
the proper split-second decisions is critical. When each 1 man

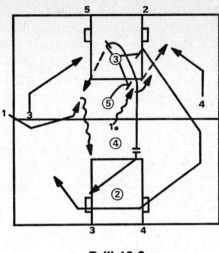

Drill 10-3

finishes his turn and is waiting for his next turn you should tell
him what his pluses and minuses were. If you have an assistant
coach, he is assigned the 3, 4, 5, and 2 players. Otherwise, you
must tell these players also. This is an excellent conditioning drill
and one the players like to run very much.

Time Sequence: In the beginning of the season we allocate ten minutes. This time is cut to seven minutes in midseason and five
minutes late in the season.

Practice Pressure: Managers count the total number of turnovers during the course of the drill. If they are above the limit established
for that particular session, the team runs sprints for each turnover
above the limit.

Drill 10-4: Five-Man Transition Break

Instructions: To start this drill the coach has the ball and will shoot,
toss it off the board, or toss it on the floor. We start the drill with
1, 2, 3, 4, and 5 men on the floor. After the rebound is secured,
the transition break is run. 4 and 3 run their streak pattern, and 2
trails 3 on the left. 5 outlets to 1. The first trip down the floor is
without defense. The second is with one defensive player. We
keep adding a player each trip until we have six. Sometimes we
include the managers on defense in this drill. The defensive
players are placed at mid-court. They run out and touch the

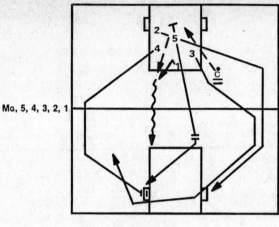

Drill 10-4

mid-court circle as the ball is rebounded. As soon as the first player touches the circle, the second may start. This procedure is followed by each player as you increase the number of players on defense. At the completion of defense they return to end of line. Rotate in a new group as the first group finishes. This is a fast-paced, continuous-motion drill.

Teaching Points: Your players must run all-out for the duration of this drill. At the same time they must fill their lanes properly, which becomes a problem when they become tired. This drill helps develop the abilities of your players to read and react to ever-changing situations. This is a must for a successful transition break. Constantly correct the mistakes of your players. We talk to them as they finish their turn before the next group starts.

Time Sequence: We work ten minutes early in the season. In mid-season and late in the season we cut the time to five minutes.

Practice Pressure: Since we are working with two or three units, the team with the fewest errors wins. The others run. The winners get a drink of water.

11

Attacking Pressing Defenses

With the Inside Power Game

CONCEPTS AGAINST ALL PRESSURE DEFENSES

Understanding the philosophy of teams using pressing defenses is a must for any team to be successful. A pressing team is first of all a risk-taking team, although at times they take calculated risks. Presses are employed by your opponent for several reasons. One reason is that the defensive team is usually trying to speed up the tempo of the game. Teams that allow the tempo to speed up generally find they are playing catch-up on the scoreboard. Another reason teams press is that they are behind and must play catch-up on the scoreboard. The lesson to be learned and remembered for dealing with pressing teams is that the pressing team hopes to force errors through the psychological havoc created by a frenzied pace. When the mind loses control, it loses control of the body. This creates a calculated risk based on percentages that the defense is willing to accept in order to create errors by the offense. Errors occur when teams become disorganized and ultimately push the panic button. The key word here for the offense to understand is *disorganization*. Preventing your team from becoming disorganized is important to your success against a pressing team. Organization of your offensive attack now becomes much more critical.

Our first objective, then, is to be highly organized in our offensive attack. We want to be under control at all times. The players must understand when they are being double teamed to remain calm and look for the open man. At this juncture of defensive pressure we are at an advantage. We are playing four on three, with 84 feet of floor space that the defense must cover with those three defensive players. Organization breeds confidence, and confidence, in turn, will negate the presses.

Our second objective is for the players to understand what the defense is attempting to force them to do. They must also understand the principles the defense uses to develop their attack. Is the defense strongest against the dribble, or should it be attacked with crisp short passes? It is questions such as these that your players must know the answers to. Are they breathing easy just because they got the ball past the ten-second line? Or are you attacking that press and trying to score against it, under control, of course? Control means being quick but not in a hurry. It means advancing the ball and obtaining the good high percentage shot, not taking the first open shot available.

ATTACKING MAN-TO-MAN FULL COURT PRESSURE

We have found over the course of past seasons that teams do not very often press us. One of the reasons might be our ability to inbound the ball so quickly in our transition game. It could be that they are worried about not getting back on defense quickly enough. Thus, the threat of your fastbreak can in itself be a deterrent. When facing a man-to-man press, we will try to beat it with our normal quick-hitting transition game, discussed in Chapter 10. The transition break is not changed against the man press.

But there are times when you will want to be very deliberate against the man press for various reasons. You might want a change of pace to control the tempo, to explode a weakness in their press, or a multitude of other things.

Against the man-to-man press we like to set up in a box formation when we're not trying to defeat it with our transition break. (See Diagram 11-1.) As in our normal game, 5 inbounds the ball against the press. We do not like to change or alter anything unless it becomes necessary. Our guards line up on the foul line at the edge of the lane. 1 is on the ball-side, with 3 opposite him. 4 lines up above the blocks on the ball-side. 2 is above the blocks opposite the ball.

Diagram 11-2 illustrates how various man-to-man presses try to attack us. What is the defense attempting to do? Are they trying to

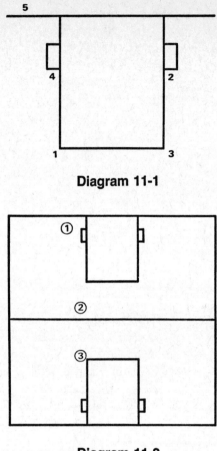

Diagram 11-1

Diagram 11-2

pressure the man inbounding and then double up on a trap situation—defensive man 1? Or are they short-stopping it to pick off the lob pass—defensive man 2? If you are beating the press deep, they will tend to place a defender in the vulnerable deep position. In our terminology they are center-fielding it. Defensive player 3 illustrates this position.

Once you beat a pressing team deep and force them to adjust to one of the previously mentioned methods to try to stop your threat, you have nullified their press. By forcing them to short-stop or center-field it, you have eliminated the possibility of double teaming. You are then operating in a five-on-four situation, with the defense deploying to a

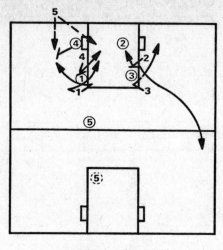

Diagram 11-3

safety position. Now attack up front, where you have a five-on-four advantage.

It doesn't matter whether the defense is short-stopping or center-fielding, we attack both positions the same way. (See Diagram 11-3.) 4 rear screens for 1, while 2 rear screens for 3. Both 1 and 3 have the option of rubbing off their screens in whatever direction is open. They must read and react to the defensive situation. After screening, 4 and 2 can step back to the ball if their defensive man tries to help out on the cutter. After screening for 3, 2 normally goes to the left side line, as in our transition break. The only time he does not is when 2 screens for 3 and then opens to the basket on a defensive switch. 5 looks to inbound his pass to 1 or 3, who are coming off their screens.

In the event 1 and 3 are unable to free themselves, 5 passes inbounds to 4 or 2. Diagram 11-4 illustrates this situation and the movement that follows. After screening for 1, 4 heads quickly toward the head of the circle and then button-hooks back to be a receiver for 5. When 5's pass is thrown inbounds to 4, 4 must be coming to meet the pass and not be caught stationary. Otherwise, the defense has the opportunity to knife through to pick off the inbounds pass. On receiving the pass, 4 immediately turns to face mid-court ready to pass to 1, 2, or 3, who are running up the sidelines. 4 then pushes the ball up the floor via the dribble, after ascertaining that his receivers are all covered.

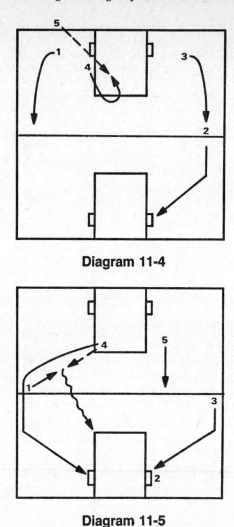

Diagram 11-4

Diagram 11-5

If 4 is double teamed, 1's responsibility is to cut back on a diagonal to be a receiver for 4. (See Diagram 11-5.) After receiving the pass, 1 pushes the ball up the floor. Meanwhile 4 has cut behind 1 and down the sideline. 5 trails to the left of 1. We are now in our transition break. It is at this point that we have actually moved into our transition break, even though our box set is used to safely inbound the ball against a man-to-man press. Diagram 11-6 illustrates how this is accomplished.

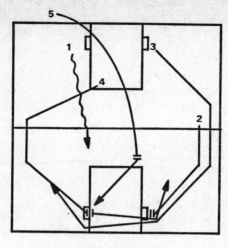

Diagram 11-6

After receiving 5's pass, 1 turns and looks first to see if 2, 4, or 3 are open before putting the ball on the floor. He then pushes the ball up the floor as quickly as possible. Meanwhile 4 and 2 have run a streak pattern to the shooting spots. 3 trails on the left side, thus reversing his role with 2, who normally trails 3. But 3 will still cross under and come out on the line of 45°. 2 stops on the blocks and screens for 4. As 3 rubs off 4's screen, 4 crosses to rub off 2's screen and comes out on the line of 45°. 5 has trailed and either has a jumper at the foul line or angles to the blocks.

What matters most when you are playing against any type of press is to maintain organization when you reach the scoring area. Many teams fail in this critical area when the good shot fails to materialize. When their good shots do not happen, your team must not panic. In our case this is taken care of since the completion of our break enters directly into the offense.

ATTACKING ZONE PRESSES

We prefer to have our team wait and set up to get the ball down court against a zone press. Our thinking here is guided by the knowledge of the hidden complexities zone presses use. Remember, to defeat any defense you must understand what it is and what it wants you to attempt. Being deliberate affords your players the opportunity to read the defensive picture. Are they facing a 1-2-1-1, 2-2-1, 2-1-2, or some other defensive set? If they know what they are facing, your players can recognize the gaps in the defense and move into them.

UTILIZE SPACE

With 84 feet of space (94 feet in college) to operate in, you should spread your players out over the entire floor. This forces the defense to spread out to cover all players. The open space must now be cut into from various angles. Remind players who are cutting to cut on sharp angles and be on the move when receiving the pass. All passes against zone presses must be short and crisp. Keep the ball in the air and not on the floor against zone presses. This is one reason we like to set up before attacking presses, particularly zones. Man-to-man presses, generally speaking, are attacked via the dribble, but only after the player looks to pass first and then uses the dribble move. When teams vary the types of presses, from zone to man-to-man or a combination of the two, your players must be under control both mentally and physically.

Defenses are defeated by attacking the heart of the defense. Against a zone press this becomes even more imperative. To advance the ball via the side-line route only helps the defense impede the forward progress of the offense. The sideline becomes an added defensive weapon as well as the time line.

Diagram 11-7 illustrates how we set up against zone presses to avoid pitfalls. We have 5 take the ball out of bounds as usual. 3 starts at the foul line area, with 4 on the ball-side foul line extended. 1 starts at the mid-court circle, with 2 deep on the blocks opposite 5's inbound position.

3 breaks either toward the ball or away from it, most of the time toward the ball. If 3 breaks to the ball, 4 breaks to the mid-court area. When 3 goes opposite the ball, 4 breaks to the ball. 5 looks to inbound the ball to either 3 or 4, depending on how he reads the defensive posture. 1 reads 3's move before he makes his move. When 3 cuts to the ball, 1 slides to his right into the open area on the backside of the press or flashes into the area vacated by 3. If 3 makes his cut away from 5, 1, after reading the defensive moves, fills 3's vacated area or slides to his left to fill the area 4 normally fills. 2 stays to the backside of the zone, ready to break in any direction to the ball but generally

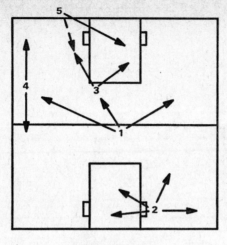

Diagram 11-7

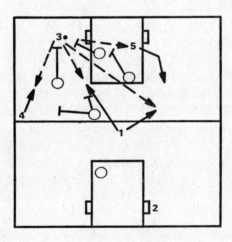

Diagram 11-8

along the baseline. After inbounding the pass, 5 trails up the left side and behind the ball.

The basic movement that follows is shown in Diagram 11-8. After 3 receives the pass, he invites the trap and immediately turns to face down court, looking at the defensive picture. I want to interject an important note here: There is a point at which the trapee must not let

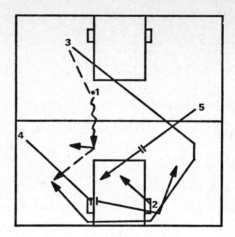

Diagram 11-9

the defenders past before he makes his pass. You will find this to be three to four feet from him. To allow defenders to come within one to two feet takes away the direct hard overhead pass. Then only the bounce pass is available. He should read from right to left, seeing whether 4, 1, or 5 is open. If 1 flashes into the middle, 5 heads up the left sideline to fill the vacant area in the backside of the zone.

If 1 receives 3's pass, he immediately turns to face down court to see if 4 or 5 is open before he puts the ball on the floor. 3 clears up the left sideline. Once penetration is made past the initial line of defense, you are generally in a four or three on one or two situation. (See Diagram 11-9.) It is at this point that your players must be disciplined enough to take the shots you want and not the hurried shots the defense wants them to take.

Some presses are willing to risk giving you the good shot, even the layup if necessary, if it will speed up the tempo to their liking. Don't think that this means they will not contest your layup attempt. But the defense will encourage you to try because they have an in- timidator waiting. Therefore, it can become a very difficult attempt and be a shot you have not practiced. In this case the percentage shot goes against you and for your opponent. This is not the situation to be caught in.

Again, we finish in the scoring area as if we were in our transition break. 4 and 3 cut on the line of 45°, with 4 pausing to screen for 3 and

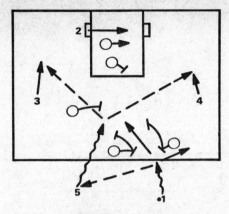

Diagram 11-10

then rubbing off 2's screen on the blocks. 5 trails 1, looking for the jumper, or, on 1's pass to 3, cuts to the blocks.

ATTACKING THE HALF COURT PRESS

Recognition of the half court trap defense by your players as the ball is being advanced into the mid-court area is critical if they are to avoid the pitfalls of this defense. Once it is determined that the defense is a half court trap, 1 must slow down and inform everyone what they are facing.

When facing a half court trap, we prefer that 1 not cross the time line and that 5 drift off to a position a little wider on his left as he trails 1 up the floor. (See Diagram 11-10.) 1 invites the trap, and if the trap doesn't develop, he penetrates into the middle, forcing two defenders to commit to him, although most of the time 1 will be trapped. At this point 1 reverses the ball to 5, who is trailing to his left. 5 now looks to penetrate into the gap created by the original trap on 1. Again, the accordian style of offense—contract and expand—is used against zone defenses. By staying in the back court, 1 is able to reverse the ball. As 5 dribble penetrates, 3 and 4 slide down the sideline, ready to receive 5's pass. On the baseline, 2 moves to the blocks opposite or flashes to the high post.

Diagram 11-11 illustrates the flash moves of 2 when the dribble penetration move is unavailable to 1 or 5. 2 flashes into the high post area as 3 and 4 cut to the basket. After receiving 1's pass, 2 turns to

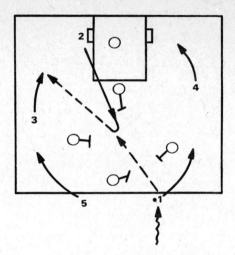

Diagram 11-11

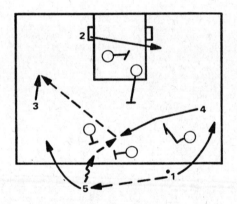

Diagram 11-12

face the basket in the direction of the area he vacated since this is the area most often open. 5 and 1 slide to the open areas in the corners.

Diagram 11-12 shows how 3 or 4 are used to flash to the high post area. When 1 reverses the ball to 5, there is generally a momentary expansion of the gap in the defense as it shifts to meet the new angle of thrust by the offense. 4 should shoot into this opening, looking for 5's bounce passes. 1 slides to the open area vacated by 4. 3 drops down the sideline as 2 crosses the lane. After making his pass to 4, 5 moves to the open area 3 vacated. 4 turns to face the basket, ready to pass to 1,

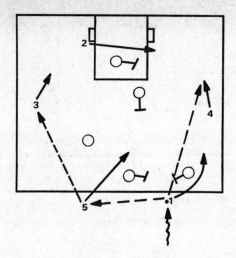

Diagram 11-13

2, or 3, whoever is open. The same options and moves apply if 3 flashes into the high post area.

When the defense is pinching in to protect the middle, 1 or 5 can pass over the top to either 3 or 4, who are dropping down in the open area of the sideline. In this instance 5 always flashes into the high post area. (See Diagram 11-13.) This same move is available to 5 when 1 reverses the ball to him. 5 passes overhead to 3 and flashes to the high post area. 1 slides to the open area above the foul line area.

Now comes the hard part. Your players must be organized and disciplined enough to determine after the first or second pass whether the defense is still trapping or has dropped back into a normal defense.

As with all aspects of our system, we teach by repetition of the fundamentals. The drills that follow are the ones we use to develop this part of our system.

Drill 11-1: Inbounds vs. Man Pressure

Instructions: Set a defense with only four players and add a fifth man later. Eventually add a sixth and a seventh defensive player. 4 and 2 set rear screens, while 1 and 3 read and react to defensive pressure. Rotate in new players at your discretion.

Teaching Points: Teach 4 and 2 to set a proper screen while reading

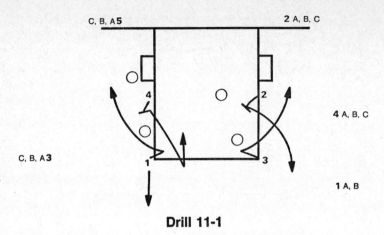

Drill 11-1

the defensive picture. Are 4's and 2's defensive players playing behind them, to the side of them, or in front of them? If they are playing in front of them, 4 and 2 should reverse pivot and simply open to the ball since they will be open. If the defensive player is fronting 1 or 3, they can run a fly pattern. Emphasize proper angle cuts on coming to meet the passes and making the correct pass for each situation.

Time Sequence: We work ten minutes early in the season. Later we cut the time to seven minutes.

Practice Pressure: The offense must inbound the ball successfully two out of three, three out of four, four out of five, five out of six times until they reach nine out of ten times. This ratio is upgraded as the season progresses. After reaching the attack zone—the mid-court area—players must decide whether to attempt to score or pull out and attack deliberately. The losers run one sprint for each time they lose.

Drill 11-2: Inbounds vs. Zone

Instructions: Set up and work against various zone sets, such as a 1-2-1-1, 2-2-1, and 2-1-2. 3 should break to the open area, while 1 and 4 read the defensive reaction to 3's cut. After inbounding, 5 trails to the left. Start this drill early in the season, using only 4 and offensive and defensive players. Later we add a fifth, sixth, and seventh defensive player.

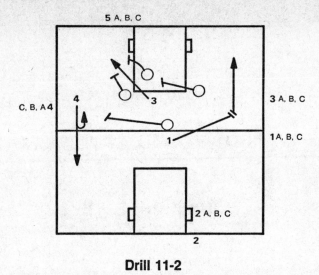

Drill 11-2

Teaching Points: Emphasize proper cutting into gaps by all players, coming to meet the passes at the proper angle, and making the correct pass for each situation. Be sure that passes are crisp and not too long. Players must turn and look up court before putting the ball on the floor. Be sure each player maintains good spacing; use the full width and length of floor.

Time Sequence: We work ten minutes during the entire season.

Practice Pressure: The offense must inbound the ball safely two out of three times, three out of four times, working up to nine out of ten times. If the defense wins, the offense must stay out and repeat until they have achieved success or fail five straight times. If they fail five straight times, they get to run with the medicine balls as many times as they failed. The defense picks up one bonus point, to be used at the conclusion of practice.

12

The Explosive

Power Game for

Situation Play

How often has the winning or losing of a game boiled down to a special situation play at the end of the game? It could be an out-of-bounds play—sideline or endline, jump balls, a free throw, deliberate fouling, or a special option to be run with ten or fewer seconds to go. Being prepared to meet these situations can make the difference between winning or losing in close games.

There are situations that occur only once or twice during a season and must be practiced for just as you would more common situations. In other words you must practice for all situations. Dire things can and do happen to the coach who waits to explain or diagram a play or situation late in the game. At this emotional moment the players cannot be expected to implement this new information anywhere near peak efficiency. Hence, a breakdown in execution often follows last-minute instruction, resulting in a game ending in frustration and emotional despair. Winning a close game with the successful use of situational play would have just the opposite effect, an extremely high psychological impact.

THE JUMP BALL

This is a situation likely to occur eight to ten times a game. It will develop at least four times at mid-court in high school, twice in college. The other times a jump ball occurs will be either at your offensive foul circle or your opponent's foul circle. You must prepare for all situations at each area. What follows are our basic rules governing these situations.

1. Play for possession when you have the obvious advantage—the best jumper.
2. Play defensively on all even jumps, but crash.
3. Play defensively in all disadvantage situations, but crash at least one or two men.
4. Always maintain an open spot for the tap; that is, a spot with no defensive players between two of yours.

Before your jumper steps in the circle, he must be certain that he is ready for the toss by the official. He must be on balance and know where he wants to tap the ball. After that he looks over the opponent's alignment and gives the signal as to where he intends to tap the ball. There are many ways to signal, but the one we prefer is by the foot he steps into the circle with. The left foot means he will tap left; the right means he will tap right.

Your jumper has now decided what he wants to try to do, but what alignment should you use? There are several basic jump-ball alignments possible.

1. Box
2. Diamond
3. T alignment
4. Special alignment

A general rule is to always match up to your opponent's alignment, unless you have adjusted for specific reasons due to a scouting report or something you picked up during the course of the game.

Another item to consider is the toss. Remember, each official has his own idiosyncrasies in tossing the balls. Does he toss it high, low, toward one player, close to himself, or away from himself? These are important considerations.

The diamond alignment is our number one selection at each jump circle. Under normal situations, with your best jumper jumping at the start of each quarter or half and tapping to your best receiver, this alignment presents the most opportunities.

Diagram 12-1 shows the mid-court tap advantage situation. In this

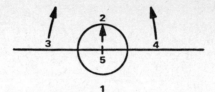

Diagram 12-1

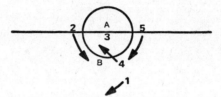

Diagram 12-2

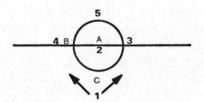

Diagram 12-3

position we try to score quickly on controlling the tap. 3 and 4, our best shooters, line up wider than normal, wide diamond, and break on the toss by the official. 5 taps to 2, who pivots and looks to pass to either 3 or 4. 2 may either pass or drive to the basket. Most teams will place a player on either side of 2, leaving 1 open for a back tap. 1 would then pass to either 3 or 4 on the sideline break or push the ball into the scoring area as quickly as possible.

Diagram 12-2 illustrates the mid-court tap disadvantage situation. In this position expect your opponent to be tapping forward. Anticipating "A" trying to tap toward "B," 2 knifes toward B as 4 pinches inside of "B." 5 can rotate either way, trying for back tap by A or a tap to left. 1 is back for defensive purposes. This is our "T" alignment.

Diagram 12-3 depicts the mid-court tap doubtful situation. We

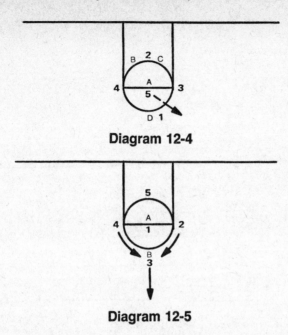

Diagram 12-4

Diagram 12-5

line up our quickest anticipator, 4, behind their side player, "B." In this case, we line up on the right-hand side of their jumper since he is right-handed. Naturally, we would line up to the left behind that player if he was left-handed. 4 knifes towards "C," their best receiver. When 4 and 1 line up behind their respective opponents, they can add a moment of indecision as to which direction they will knife through to. We try to tap to 5.

Let us look now at a tap at your basket in which the advantage is yours. (See Diagram 12-4.) In this situation the defense is forced to double team your best receiver, 2, who is facing the jumper. This allows you the opportunity to tip to where two of your players, 1 and 3, who do not have an opponent between them, are open.

When you are jumping at your basket in the disadvantage position—one of your smaller players jumping against a taller player—a defensive tap is dictated. (See Diagram 12-5.) Your jumper should try to legally impede his opponent's tap. Generally in this position, your opponent will tap forward. With this knowledge, your wings, 4 and 2, should knife toward their best receiver, "B." 3 is responsible for protecting against the quick break. If 1 is able to gain control of the tap, he taps to the open area between opponents.

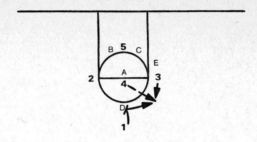

Diagram 12-6

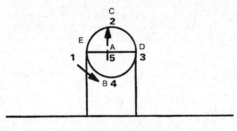

Diagram 12-7

Diagram 12-6 illustrates the doubtful tap situation at your basket. Again, your opponents must double team your top receiver, 5. 4, the jumper, should try to tap to the area between his own two players, 1 and 3. 1 seals his man, and 3 goes for the tap.

The story is entirely different when the jump ball is being contested at the opponent's basket. Diagram 12-7 illustrates this situation when the advantage is yours. Place your best receiver facing your jumper. In this case 2 is the designated receiver. 3 and 1 line up on the inside positions of their opponents. 1 rotates to help 4 out on "B." You must protect your defensive position even when you have the advantage.

When the ball is being jumped at the disadvantage position at your opponent's basket, it is imperative to protect your defensive basket even if it means giving up the back tap. Whatever happens, you do not want your opponent to tap it forward and thereby set up a quick score. Place your two best non-jumping receivers, 5 and 2, at the inside defensive position. This forces your opponent to take a wider position. Next, have 3 and 4 take outside positions at the center lane and pinch in

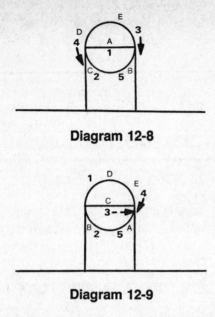

Diagram 12-8

Diagram 12-9

if your opponent obtains a more advantageous position. By doing this, you force them to tap away and thus take away the easy shot. When in this position, all players must be extremely aggressive and try to deflect the ball in any direction and come up with the ball in the scramble for it. (See Diagram 12-8.) Because your opponent will often back tap in this situation, you might gamble and have 3 and 4 knife inside toward "E."

Perhaps the toughest of all jump-ball situations is the doubtful tap at your opponent's basket. A mistake here results in a quick two points for your opponent. 5 and 2 must take the inside defensive position if you fail to control the tap. If 3 can control the tap, he should try to tap toward the side of the opponent's slowest player. This will give you a better opportunity to obtain 3's tap. (See Diagram 12-9.)

OUT-OF-BOUNDS PLAY

The most important objective here is to inbound the ball safely. Your next objective is to get the ball to your best shooter for a high percentage shot. You should always have your best passer inbound the ball. Take into consideration rebounding assignments and always have your two best rebounders in rebounding position. On all out-of-bounds plays you must protect yourself defensively by assigning a player to this important area.

Due to the time limit of five seconds from the time the official hands the ball to your player, all players must hustle to their positions. Your inbounder must be back as far from the sideline or endline as possible. This affords him a better view of the defensive picture without pressure from his man.

We designate all inbound plays by a number to help facilitate what option is going to be run with a minimum of verbage. In order to obtain the best results, a team must repeat each play as often as possible in practice. Rotate players to all positions and teach each option to every player. The time needed for this will be well spent.

SIDELINE INBOUNDS PLAY

We use one basic sideline play from the mid-court area in which options are used according to the positioning of the defensive players. Diagram 12-10 illustrates the sideline inbound play. 3, second guard, inbounds the ball at all times on the sideline. Our reasoning here is that the inbounder is most often the easiest player to get a return pass to. He

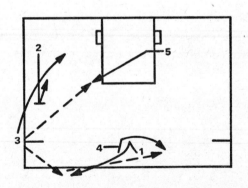

Diagram 12-10

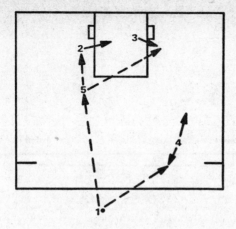

Diagram 12-11

is our best shooter as well as a top passer. 2 starts in the near baseline corner to be a receiver for 3's pass, and if he doesn't receive a pass as he comes toward the ball, he sets a screen on 3's defensive man. 5 flashes to the high post area. He will come as high as he has to in order to get open. 3's first priority is to make his inbound pass to 5, 2, and then 1. 4 screens for 1, who sets up his man and then cuts back court. This is a must when he is inbounding the ball near the mid-court time line. It eliminates the possibility of a back court violation as well as a double team situation by the defense in the mid-court corner.

When the ball is inbounded to 1, he looks quickly to 5, who is in the high post area, or 4, who has looped around to be a receiver for 1's pass. After receiving 1's pass, 5 turns to look inside immediately. (See Diagram 12-11.) If 3 or 2 cutting hard to the basket is open, 5 makes his pass inside. If 1 makes his pass to 4, 4 looks to 3 or 2 cutting. 5 and 2 rebound on the blocks, with 3 and 4 rebounding on the line of 45°. 1 is deep safety.

Because 5 flashes high, many teams will front him, trying to deny his flash move. 3 and 5 must recognize this defensive move and use the over-the-top pass. 5 fakes his flash move and then seals his defensive man on his hip with his lead hand high, looking for 3's pass. (See Diagram 12-12.)

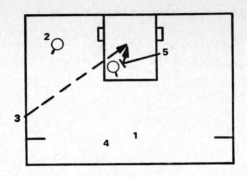

Diagram 12-12

ENDLINE INBOUNDS PLAY

Remember, the positioning of the defensive players will determine the option or play to be run. We are trying to get the ball inbounds to our best shooter with a minimal number of passes, one if possible.

Our designated number one play is shown in Diagram 12-13. 1, our point guard, is responsible for inbounding the ball. All movement starts as 1 takes the ball from the official. 2, 5, 4, and 3 line up single file in that order, with 2 starting at a spot above the blocks. 3 jab steps to the inside and then cuts for the corner, rubbing off 4's brush screen. 3 immediately looks for his shot or to pass inside. 4 and 5 set a double screen on 3's defensive man. 2 cuts for the basket, looking for the quick pass. After screening, 5 flashes for the lob pass from 1, to screen 1's defensive man, or to post up for 3's pass inside, in that sequence. 4 loops back, after screening for 3, to be a safety or to receive 1's deep pass. 3 may tap 4, letting him know that 4 is to cut to the corner; 3 is then safety.

Diagram 12-14 continues the number 1 inbounds play. After passing to 3, 1 rubs off 5's screen, looking for a quick pass and taking his jump shot. 5 posts up after rear-screening 1's defensive man. 1 may call any player's number to indicate that the player is to break to the corner.

Inbounds play number two is shown in Diagram 12-15. This play is a variation of our number 1 play and is used whenever the defense

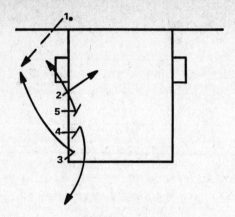

Diagram 12-13

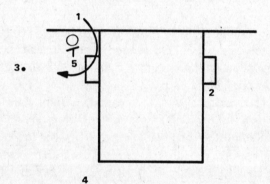

Diagram 12-14

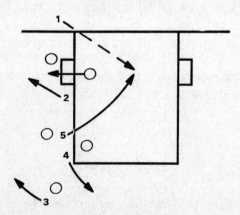

Diagram 12-15

attempts to defend this formation by placing a man to the outside of one of our players in the line. 3, on top, widens up his position, while 4 rotates deep, as usual, taking his man with him. 2 cuts to the corner, pulling his defender with him. Now 5 has the inside area cleared for him. 1 inbounds to 5 with either a lob or a bounce pass.

Many teams will zone us on endline situations. In this case we always run our 1 play. The only difference is that each player is breaking into the seam of the zone. When teams zone they are saying you will not get the inside shot but you can have the outside shot. Therefore, it is much easier to successfully inbound the ball, but you will have more difficulty obtaining as high a percentage shot.

LAST SHOT PLAY, ENDLINE BACKCOURT

There are several important things involved here. The first is what type of defense they are using. The second is how much time is left to play. If your opponents are behind, they must press. If they do this, we box since this is our normal procedure against presses (see Chapter 11). If the score is tied or you are behind, a tight press by your opponent is not likely to be used. In this situation it is advisable to pass inbounds near mid-court and call time out. With three to five seconds left, there is ample time for this maneuver. If there are less than two seconds and no time outs left, you must try for the bomb. (See Diagram 12-16.)

Your fastest player takes the ball out of bounds, but he should also be one of your best shooters. If you have to compromise, select the shooter. The other players line up opposite the side of the lane in a single line. 2 is on top, with 5, 4, and 1 next. 1 steps out of bounds to receive 3's pass as 2 and 5 cut to 3, looking as though they are coming to meet the pass. 4 jab steps and cuts around 2 and 5 to the mid-court area as secondary receiver. 3 runs a fly pattern, rubbing off 2's and 5's brush screen. 1 leads 3 deep or hits his secondary receiver if he is covered.

TIME OUTS

A coach must decide when his team will call a time out. You must have a general method for all called time outs. Our rule is that the coach will always call the first time out. This prevents a misuse of your

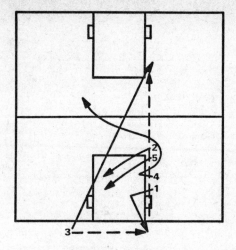

Diagram 12-16

precious time outs. We like to save, if possible, four time outs for late in the game.

Players and coaches must always be alert to the number of time outs that each team has remaining. Games have been lost because a team was unaware of the number of time outs its opponent had left.

What happens when a time out is called? How do your players arrive at the bench and what procedures are followed? Remember, your time is very limited and must not be wasted. Diagram 12-17 illustrates how we want our players to sit and how our bench players are to place themselves. Our 1 man takes the center seat, with 5 and 3 to his left and 2 and 4 to his right. The bench is lined up by position opposite the playing five. The head coach is in the middle, with the assistant at the end nearest the scorer's table. If there is a question dealing with the scorer's table, your assistant coach can be right there.

In summary, I have described our entire system for playing inside power basketball, our philosophy and the theories responsible for the development of this system.

I believe that basketball is a team game and not a one-on-one contest. With a team concept and an opportunity for all players to score, a coach decreases morale and discipline problems. In return, this builds team spirit and pride.

Remember, there is no easy method for winning basketball

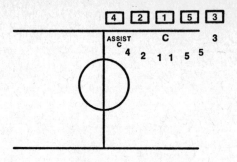

Diagram 12-17

games, just hard work. This system requires strict attention to detail in practice and repeated drilling on fundamentals. We try to leave nothing to chance since the pressure of big games will bring out any flaws in your players. This is why our practice drills are designed to condition our players to the style of play we want. We practice hard to enable our players to respond automatically to each and every situation that arises. What I am trying to say is that we believe our inside power game is flexible enough to take advantage of and obtain the high percentage shot as the game is played today and will be in the future.

Index